KU-776-736

Homosexuality, Masculinity & Femininity

Edited by
Michael W. Ross

Homosexuality, Masculinity & Femininity was originally published in 1983 by The Haworth Press, Inc., under the title *Homosexuality and Social Sex Roles*. It has also been published as *Journal of Homosexuality,* Volume 9, Number 1, Fall 1983.

Harrington Park Press
New York • Binghamton

ISBN 0-918393-04-3

Published by

Harrington Park Press, Inc.
28 East 22 Street
New York, New York 10010

Harrington Park Press, Inc., is a subsidiary of The Haworth Press, Inc., 28 East 22 Street, New York, New York 10010.

Homosexuality, Masculinity & Femininity was originally published in 1983 by The Haworth Press, Inc., under the title *Homosexuality and Social Sex Roles.* It has also been published as *Journal of Homosexuality,* Volume 9, Number 1, Fall 1983.

© 1985 by Harrington Park Press, Inc. All rights reserved. No part of this work may be reproduced or utilized in any form or by any means, electronic or mechanical including photocopying, microfilm and recording, or by any information storage and retrieval system without permission in writing from The Haworth Press, Inc., 28 East 22 Street, New York, New York 10010. Printed in the United States of America.

Library of Congress Cataloging in Publication Data

Homosexuality and social sex roles.
    Homosexuality, masculinity & femininity.

    Reprint. Originally published: Homosexuality and social sex roles. New York : Haworth Press, c1983. (Research on homosexuality ; no. 7)
    Originally also published as journal of homosexuality, v. 9, no. 1, fall, 1983.
    Includes bibliographies.
    1. Homosexuality. 2. Sex role. 3. Social role. I. Ross, Michael W., 1952- . II. Title.
III. Title: Homosexuality, masculinity and femininity.
HQ76.25.H675   1985   306.7'66   84-19778
ISBN 0-918393-04-3 (pbk.)

CONTENTS

The *Journal of Homosexuality* is devoted to theoretical, empirical, and historical research on homosexuality, heterosexuality, sexual identity, social sex roles, and the sexual relationships of both men and women. It was created to serve the allied disciplinary and professional groups represented by psychology, sociology, history, anthropology, biology, medicine, the humanities, and law. Its purposes are:

  a) to bring together, within one contemporary scholarly journal, theoretical, empirical, and historical research on human sexuality, particularly sexual identity;
  b) to serve as a forum for scholarly research of heuristic value for the understanding of human sexuality, based not only in the more traditional social or biological sciences, but also in literature, history and philosophy;
  c) to explore the political, social, and moral implications of research on human sexuality for professionals, clinicians, social scientists, and scholars in a wide variety of disciplines and settings.

EDITOR

JOHN P. De CECCO, PhD, *Professor of Psychology and Director, Center for Research and Education in Sexuality (CERES), San Francisco State University*

MANUSCRIPT EDITOR

WENDELL RICKETTS, *Center for Research and Education in Sexuality*

ASSOCIATE EDITORS

STUART KELLOGG, MONIKA KEHOE, and MICHAEL G. SHIVELY, *Center for Research and Education in Sexuality*

FOUNDING EDITOR

CHARLES SILVERSTEIN, *Institute for Human Identity, New York City*

EDITORIAL BOARD

ROGER AUSTEN, *Teaching Fellow, University of Southern California, Los Angeles*
ALAN BELL, PhD, *Department of Counseling, Indiana University*
PHILIP W. BLUMSTEIN, PhD, *Associate Professor of Sociology, University of Washington*
VERN L. BULLOUGH, PhD, *Dean, Faculty of Natural and Social Sciences, State University of New York College, Buffalo*
ELI COLEMAN, PhD, *Assistant Professor and Coordinator of Clinical Services, Program in Human Sexuality, University of Minnesota*
LOUIE CREW, PhD, *Associate Professor of English, University of Wisconsin, Stevens Point*
LOUIS CROMPTON, PhD, *Professor of English, University of Nebraska, Lincoln*
MARTIN DANNECKER, PhD, *Abteilung für Sexualwissenschaft, Klinikum der Johann Wolfgang Goethe Universität, Frankfurt am Main, West Germany*
JOSHUA DRESSLER, JD, *Professor of Law, Wayne State University Law School*
LILLIAN FADERMAN, PhD, *Professor of English, California State University, Fresno*
BYRNE R. S. FONE, PhD, *Associate Professor of English, The City College, City University of New York*
JOHN GAGNON, PhD, *Professor of Sociology, State University of New York at Stony Brook*
JOHN GONSIOREK, PhD, *Clinical Psychologist, Twin Cities Therapy Clinic, Minneapolis, Minnesota; Clinical Assistant Professor, Department of Psychology, University of Minnesota*
ERWIN HAEBERLE, PhD, *Director of Historical Research, Institute for the Advanced Study of Human Sexuality, San Francisco*

RICHARD HALL, MA, *Writer, New York City*

JOEL D. HENCKEN, MA, *Private Practice, Boston; PhD Candidate in Clinical Psychology, University of Michigan*

EVELYN HOOKER, PhD, *Retired Research Professor, Psychology Department, University of California, Los Angeles*

RICHARD J. HOFFMAN, PhD, *Associate Professor, Department of History, San Francisco State University*

FRED KLEIN, MD, *Clinical Institute for Human Relationships, San Diego*

MARY RIEGE LANER, PhD, *Associate Professor of Sociology, Arizona State University, Tempe*

ELLEN LEWIN, PhD, *Medical Anthropology Program, University of San Francisco*

DON LILES, MA, *Instructor in English, City College of San Francisco*

A. P. MACDONALD, JR., PhD, *Acting Director and Associate Professor, Center for the Family, University of Massachusetts, Amherst*

WILLIAM F. OWEN, MD, *Private Practice, San Francisco*

L. ANNE PEPLAU, PhD, *Associate Professor of Psychology, University of California, Los Angeles*

KENNETH PLUMMER, PhD, *Department of Sociology, University of Essex, England*

SHARON RAPHAEL, PhD, *Associate Professor of Sociology, California State University, Dominguez Hills*

KENNETH READ, PhD, *Professor of Anthropology, University of Washington, Seattle*

MICHAEL ROSS, PhD, *Senior Demonstrator in Psychiatry, The Flinders University of South Australia, Adelaide, Australia*

DOROTHY SEIDEN, PhD, *Professor, Department of Home Economics, San Francisco State University*

G. WILLIAM SKINNER, PhD, *Professor of Anthropology, Stanford University*

RICHARD W. SMITH, PhD, *Professor of Psychology, California State University, Northridge*

JOHN P. SPIEGEL, MD, *Director, Training Program in Ethnicity and Mental Health, Brandeis University; Current President, American Academy of Psychoanalysis*

FREDERICK SUPPE, PhD, *Chair, Committee on the History and Philosophy of Science, University of Maryland, College Park*

JOHN UNGARETTI, MA, *Classics; MA, Literature; San Francisco*

JEFFREY WEEKS, PhD, *Research Fellow, Department of Sociology, University of Essex, England*

JAMES WEINRICH, PhD, *Psychiatry and Behavioral Sciences, Johns Hopkins University*

JACK WIENER, MSW, *Retired, National Institute of Mental Health, Bethesda, Maryland*

DEBORAH WOLF, PhD, *Institute for the Study of Social Change, University of California, Berkeley*

WAYNE S. WOODEN, PhD, *Assistant Professor, Behavioral Science, California State Polytechnic University, Pomona*

Foreword

The association of femininity with male homosexual relationships is at least as old as Greek classical culture. Then it was believed that the partner who enacted the role of receiver in anal copulation, especially if this was a habitual and exclusive practice of an older citizen, surrendered a large measure of his masculinity. The assumption of the female coital role, it was believed, replaced masculinity with femininity. Apart from the slight tarnish to one's masculinity that could accrue as a result of taking a receiver role, partners in Greek homosexual relationships—fellow warriors or adventurers, for example—could be seen as masculine.

The nineteenth-century creation of the idea of sexual identity, as reflected in the writing of Karl Heinrich Ulrichs, focused from the start on the issues of femininity and masculinity. Urnings, according to Ulrichs, were unique human specimens: As females they had a masculine drive lodged in female sexual organs and as males a feminine drive mysteriously embodied in male organs. In their sexual relationships they hoped for the "natural" complementarity of femininity and masculinity that was sought by heterosexual partners. For over one hundred years, psychiatry, reflecting this early formulation of the idea of the homosexual identity, continued to assume that "homosexual" males were deficient in masculinity, the females in femininity, and both perhaps embarrassingly proficient in the traits associated with their opposite sexes.

As the research presented in this symposium on homosexuality and sex roles ably reveals, the issues of femininity and masculinity remain central to the discourse on homosexuality. Some of the authors report that the putative lack of masculinity in homosexual males may be biological in origin, perhaps traceable to inadequate fetal androgenization of the brain and recrudescent in the poor childhood relationships of fathers and sons. Most of the authors, however, see the inadequacy in the culture or in societal attitudes towards individuals identified as homosexuals. The guest editor, in his own research report, provides evidence that, while some homosexual males can be shown to be less masculine than others, the diminished masculinity can be traced to the rigid enforcement of masculine stereotypes and sexual intolerance. In fact, as another article demonstrates, the degree of intolerance is directly related to the prevalence of traditional sex-role attitudes. Even

© 1983 by The Haworth Press, Inc. All rights reserved.

men who identify themselves as homosexuals, as shown by one symposiast, apply the same stereotypes as their heterosexual counterparts in assessing masculinity in fellow males.

The women, as is often the case in studies of femininity and masculinity, appear considerably less harried by sex-role stereotypes. In their sexual relationships they appear to transcend the established definitions of biological sex, sex roles, and sexual orientation and select partners on the basis of personality.

At a more general level, as one author hints, it may be that femininity and masculinity are crude labels for the complicated intermeshing of beliefs about what it is to be a female or a male. It is the *beliefs* about biological sex, not the brute biological fact itself, that may reveal the structure of sexual relationships, regardless of whether they are heterosexual or homosexual.

I want to express my deepest appreciation to Michael Ross, the guest editor of this symposium, for attracting as contributors a most distinguished roster of scholars. I want to thank the contributors, almost all of whom are making their debut in the *Journal* with this issue, for collectively showing many conceptual facets of and several approaches to the study of sex roles and sexual orientation. I am especially pleased that the contributors are from three continents, and even more countries, since it is the hope of the *Journal* to be increasingly international in scope.

John P. De Cecco, PhD

Homosexuality, Masculinity & Femininity

INTRODUCTION

Homosexuality and Social Sex Roles: A Re-Evaluation

Michael W. Ross, PhD

The Flinders University of South Australia Medical School

The relationship of social sex role (masculinity or femininity) to homosexuality has for a long time been assumed to be a necessary, if not a sufficient, one. Historical evidence, however, does not always support such a contention. Bullough (1976), for example, suggests that the association of masculinity or femininity with male homosexuality has had some relationship to the position of women in a particular society, and McIntosh (1968) suggests that for English-speaking societies at least, the homosexual role as currently perceived (homosexual men as effeminate and homosexual women as masculine) developed only in the 18th century.

The association between male homosexuality and femininity in scientific investigation can be traced at least as far back as the 19th century. Ulrichs, as reported by Ellis and Symonds (1897), maintained that in male inverts (homosexuals) a female soul existed within a male body. In 1886, von Krafft-Ebing indicated that homosexuality resulted from the individual's possessing "traces of psychical hermaphroditism": Male homosexuals had a female mind, the mind of the "sex to which an individual by instinct, belongs." Ellis and Symonds, while stating that this "merely crystallizes into an epigram the superficial impression of the matter" (p. 132), replace this with an equivalent biological explanation by suggesting that, in the homosexual, the development process has not proceeded normally, resulting in an excess of cells of

Dr. Ross is Senior Demonstrator, Department of Psychiatry, The Flinders University of South Australia Medical School, Bedford Park, S.A. 5042, Australia.

© 1983 by The Haworth Press, Inc. All rights reserved.

1

the opposite sex. Such reasoning, which unquestioningly transfers the homosexual role to the organic level, is still apparent in the basic hypotheses tested in biological studies of homosexuals. Many of these hypotheses appear to assume that homosexuality contains, as a necessary etiological ingredient, a gender identity of the opposite sex, manifest as deviant social sex role.

Such hypotheses may be questioned on several levels. Kuhn (1970) argues that science tends to test hypotheses within particular paradigms, but does not test the assumptions of the paradigms themselves. Paradigms, suggests Kuhn, provide model problems and solutions to a community of scientists. Hypotheses are generated within these paradigms that provide both the closest fit with empirical data and maximum internal coherence. The result is what he describes as "a strenuous and devoted attempt to force nature into the conceptual boxes supplied by professional education" (p. 5). When anomalies occur that call these boxes into question, a new paradigm develops. New theory requires the reconstruction of prior theory and the re-evaluation of prior fact.

Kuhn's view of science as a succession of paradigms applies as much to the study of sexuality as to physical or biological science. It could be argued, for example, that most studies of homosexuality have set about to test the 19th-century model of same-sex preference whose hypothesis it is that a homosexual individual contains psychological (via gender identity and parental identification) or biological (via brain differentiation) elements of the opposite sex. Researchers such as Ross, Rogers and McCulloch (1978) have suggested that seeing male homosexuals as individuals with a cross-gender identification is equivalent to saying that because society considers sexual interaction natural or acceptable only between different-sex partners, a male who wishes to interact sexually with another male must think of himself as, or contain attributes of, a female. Scott (1972) has also suggested that hypotheses tested reflect social consensus rather than any other perception of social reality. He goes on to argue that the validity of such hypotheses is "proven" every time we use the categories of perception in which the hypotheses are embedded.

Similar comments have been made in other fields of research. Strathearn (1976), for example, makes the point that sex differences in behavior are not just the results of biological, psychological and societal interactions, but that gender constructs endure because of their usefulness as symbols in society. Similarly, Cucchiari (1981) argues that marriage affirms, defines and reproduces gender duality, and that this serves the function of placing all human relationships and activities within a rigid two-gender system. Thus, the preoccupation with maleness or femaleness in research on homosexuality may be a function more of their overriding importance as symbols in constructing our social reality than of any relationship between the two concepts. Evidence cited by Whitehead (1981) indicates that in some tribal societies homosexuality may be regarded as providing masculinity (e.g., New Guinea), while in others it may imply femininity (e.g., native North America). Each rests on a different cultural construction of sex and gender. While it may be posited, then, that investigation of homosexuality utilizing the constructs of maleness and femaleness is based upon common social constructions of sexuality, particularly gender, the relationship of homosexuality, gender identity and social sex role has often been confused.

Freund, Nagler, Langevin, Zajac and Steiner (1974) questioned the appropriateness of measuring gender identity with common psychometric masculinity-femininity tests. Using a new test that incorporated feminine gender identity items with high face validity, and testing transsexual, heterosexual and homosexual males, they found that the heterosexual and homosexual groups overlapped considerably, and that the transsexual group did not overlap with the heterosexual cases. They concluded that sex object preference (heterosexuality or homosexuality) and gender identity are to a considerable degree independent, and that if both are disturbed, the resulting individual will be both transsexual *and* homosexual. Shively and De Cecco (1977) also define sexual orientation and gender identity as potentially separate entities. Such findings have not, however, prevented some researchers from classifying homosexuality as a disorder of gender identity.

The difficulty has probably arisen from the fact that social sex roles and gender identity (the sense of being a male or a female) are usually highly correlated, and because social sex roles are assumed to measure the intervening variable of gender identity. It is therefore critical that variables such as sex object preference, social sex role, and gender identity not be confused. This point is elaborated by Shively and De Cecco.

In turn, separation of these constructs raises questions about whether feminine role in male homosexuals and masculine role in female homosexuals are a necessary concomitant of homosexuality. Over the past decade, results have conflicted, although some of the confusion may be a function of the use of scales whose validity criteria and underlying assumptions (e.g., unicontinual or bicontinual measures of social sex role) have been quite different. However, when we ask whether the relationship of social sex role and homosexuality is one of homosexuality causing deviant social sex role, deviant social sex role causing homosexuality, something else causing both, or no necessary relationship, the varying approaches may be differentiated.

The view that homosexuality is associated with deviant social sex role implies that all homosexuals will contain attributes of the opposite sex. It is clear from past research, however, that there is little agreement on this; some studies show confirmatory evidence and others report no differences. It appears reasonable to assume that the association of deviant social sex role with homosexuality is not invariable. West (1977), however, has commented that test scores on scales measuring masculinity and femininity are largely determined by superficial attributes that could be the by-products of a homosexual lifestyle rather than a cause of homoerotic orientation. Similarly, studies of excessively feminine boys have indicated that while about 56% on follow-up are homosexual, slightly less than half are not (Grellert, Newcomb & Bentler, 1982). On the other hand, a large literature suggests that homosexuals in many cultures demonstrate childhood play patterns typical of the opposite sex (Grellert et al., 1982; Whitam, 1977). While Ross's (1980) data suggest that this may be a function of retrospective distortion in line with societal expectation of the homosexual role, the wide variety of reports of cross-sex play in homosexuals cannot be explained in terms of this alone.

However, the concept of homosexuality across cultures creates some problems in interpretation. Carrier's (1980) data show that what is considered homosexuality in Anglo-Saxon society (sexual relations with another male) is different from what is considered homosexuality in Mediterranean-based cultures (taking a "passive" role in relations with another male: There is no stigma attached to "active" same-sex relations). Ross et al. (1978) suggest that societal factors may play a large part in the relationship between homosexuality and social sex role because homosexuals, on identifying themselves as homosexual, may accept the conventional expectation that they will be feminine if they are male and masculine if they are female. In such a societal analysis, attention is focused not on the deviant gender identity or social sex role, but onto the societal constructions of sexuality that lead to such hypotheses. This is not to say that there is no merit in testing other hypotheses, but that given the lack of empirical evidence of a consistent relationship between social sex role and homosexuality, it is important to understand the more subtle aspects of the relationship that may stem from social or cultural assumptions.

Previous research has generally concentrated on *cause* rather than *process* in terms of this relationship. Given that unifactorial explanations have not been forthcoming, one of the hopes in putting together a special issue on homosexuality and social sex roles was that a reevaluation of the area might be possible, both through testing critical assumptions of previous approaches or by laying the foundations for new ones.

What are fruitful avenues for researching the relationships between homosexuality, masculinity and femininity? Excluding for the moment biological research, which mainly approaches the area from an etiological or etiological-interactionist perspective, it seems reasonable to note that previous work may have been a function of being limited to one paradigm of homosexuality and social interaction. Future research might concentrate on the basis of homosexual attraction, rather than on the sex of the partner. As Gagnon and Simon (1973) noted a decade ago, "We have allowed the object choice of the homosexual to dominate our imagery of him." Little is known of the attitudinal and belief systems of homosexuals themselves, or of public expectations of homosexuals and their roles. Cross-culturally, the meaning of the term homosexual is not congruent, nor are many of the facets of what is considered masculine or feminine. For that matter, there is some doubt even in the English-speaking scientific community whether various measures of social sex role assess similar facets of behavior or attitudes.

In summary, it seems fair to conclude that while we have established that homosexuality and deviant social sex roles are not necessary or sufficient causes of one another, biological, psychological, familial, and societal factors are not well understood in this relationship. Movement away from a focus on the gender of homosexual individuals to other bases of attraction, societal expectations and roles, and attitudes of homosexuals toward social sex roles, is probably critical to future research in this area. It is hoped that the papers that comprise this special issue will go some way toward illuminating the relationships between homosexuality and social sex roles, and toward generating further hypotheses for empirical investigation. Above all, sexological paradigms that influence findings at the level of initial hypotheses and selection of research questions must be made clear, so that we can avoid testing only within such paradigms and not between them.

REFERENCES

Bullough, V. L. *Sexual variance in society and history.* Chicago: University of Chicago Press, 1976.

Carrier, J. Homosexual behavior in cross-cultural perspective. In J. Marmor (Ed.), *Homosexual behavior: A modern reappraisal.* New York: Basic Books, 1980.

Cucchiari, S. The gender revolution and the transition from bisexual horde to patrilocal band: The origins of gender hierarchy. In S. B. Ortner & H. Whitehead (Eds.), *Sexual meanings: The cultural construction of gender and sexuality.* Cambridge: Cambridge University Press, 1981.

Ellis, H. & Symonds, J. A. *Sexual inversion.* New York: Arno Press, 1975. (Originally published, 1897.)

Freund, K. W., Nagler, E., Langevin, R., Zajac, A. & Steiner, B. Measuring feminine gender identity in homosexual males. *Archives of Sexual Behavior,* 1974, *3*, 249-260.

Gagnon, J. H. & Simon, W. *Sexual conduct: The social sources of human sexuality.* Chicago: Aldine, 1973.

Grellert, E. A., Newcomb, M. D. & Bentler, P. M. Childhood play activities of male and female homosexuals and heterosexuals. *Archives of Sexual Behavior,* 1982, *11*, 451-478.

Krafft-Ebing, R. von. *Psychopathia sexualis.* (H. E. Wedeck, trans.). New York: G. P. Putnam's Sons, 1965. (Originally published, 1886.)

Kuhn, T. *The Structure of scientific revolutions*. (2nd ed.). Chicago: University of Chicago Press, 1970.

McIntosh, M. The homosexual role. *Social Problems*, 1968, *16*, 182-192.

Ross, M. W. Retrospective distortion in homosexual research. *Archives of Sexual Behavior*, 1980, *9*, 523-531.

Ross, M. W., Rogers, L. J. & McCulloch, H. Stigma, sex and society: A new look at gender differentiation and sexual variation. *Journal of Homosexuality*, 1978, *3*, 315-330.

Scott, R. A. A proposed framework for analyzing deviance as a property of social order. In R. A. Scott & J. D. Douglas (Eds.), *Theoretical perspectives on deviance*. New York: Basic Books, 1972.

Shively, M. G. & De Cecco, J. P. Components of sexual identity. *Journal of Homosexuality*, 1977, *3*, 41-48.

Strathearn, M. An anthropological perspective. In B. B. Lloyd & J. Archer (Eds.), *Exploring sex differences*. London: Academic Press, 1976.

West, D. J. *Homosexuality re-examined*. London: Duckworth, 1977.

Whitam, F. L. Childhood indicators of male homosexuality. *Archives of Sexual Behavior*, 1977, *6*, 89-96.

Whitehead, H. The bow and the burden strap: A new look at institutionalized homosexuality in native North America. In S. B. Ortner & H. Whitehead (Eds.), *Sexual meanings: The cultural construction of gender and sexuality*. Cambridge: Cambridge University Press, 1981.

Is the Distant Relationship of Fathers and Homosexual Sons Related to the Sons' Erotic Preference for Male Partners, or to the Sons' Atypical Gender Identity, or to Both?

Kurt Freund, MD, DSc
Ray Blanchard, PhD
Clarke Institute of Psychiatry

ABSTRACT. Study 1 compared the retrospectively reported father-son relationships of four groups of adult males: (a) Gynephiles (males who erotically prefer physically mature females), (b) androphiles (who prefer physically mature males), (c) a combined group of heterosexual pedophiles and pedohebephiles (the latter being attracted to pubescent as well as prepubescent females), and (d) a combined group of homosexual pedophiles and pedohebephiles (the latter attracted to pubescent as well as prepubescent males). The gynephiles were paid volunteers; the latter three groups were patients. The androphiles, the only group among those compared known to exhibit a measurably greater degree of cross gender identity in childhood, were also the only group to report significantly poorer father-son relations. The homosexual pedo/pedohebephiles, who also prefer male partners but who exhibit typical male gender identity in childhood, did not differ in father-son relations from the gynephiles or the heterosexual pedo/pedohebephiles. Study 2 showed that, within a sample of nonpatient volunteer androphiles, those individuals who reported the greatest degree of cross gender behavior in childhood also tended to report the worst relationships with their fathers. This correlation was replicated within a sample of androphilic patients in Study 3. The consistent pattern of results obtained from these three studies suggests that the emotionally distant relationships of fathers and andro-

Dr. Freund is Head, Department of Behavioural Sexology, Clarke Institute of Psychiatry, Toronto, Canada, and Consultant in Sexology, Ontario Correctional Institute, Brampton, Canada. Dr. Blanchard is affiliated with the Gender Identity Clinic, Clarke Institute of Psychiatry, Toronto, Canada.

These studies were supported by Ontario Mental Health Foundation Grant No. 809 to K. Freund. Requests for reprints should be sent to Kurt Freund, Research Section of Behavioural Sexology, Clarke Institute of Psychiatry, 250 College Street, Toronto, Ontario, Canada M5T 1R8.

The authors wish to thank Kent Campbell, Freda Salutin, Cathy Spegg, and Kenneth Zucker for their various and valuable contributions to this paper.

© 1983 by The Haworth Press, Inc. All rights reserved.

7

philic sons relate to the sons' atypical childhood gender identity (or observable gender role behavior) rather than to the sons' erotic preference for male partners *per se*.

Retrospective studies of adult male heterosexuals and homosexuals have quite consistently yielded two findings. First, adult homosexual males are more likely to report poor (i.e., distant if not antagonistic) childhood relationships with their fathers. Second, homosexual males are more likely to report an integrated pattern of cross gender behavior in childhood. In the present paper, we will use the term *feminine gender identity* to refer to a hypothetical attribute inferred from such patterning, i.e., covariation, of observable cross sex-typed behaviors.

The present studies were an attempt to investigate the triangular relationship among these three variables: Sex-of-partner preference (heterosexuality vs. homosexuality), father-son interpersonal distance, and childhood gender identity (or observable gender behavior). More specifically, the question was: Is the emotional distance between fathers and homosexual sons related to the sons' erotic preference for male partners, or to the sons' atypical gender identity (or observable gender role behavior), or to both?

Historical background. Freud, at least at one time, and many of his followers believed that a male child's relationships with his parents are decisive factors in his becoming heterosexual or homosexual, and that the presence or absence of a suitable father model is of particular importance for his development toward heterosexuality or homosexuality (Allen, 1940, 1952, 1958, 1962; Ferenczi, 1914/1963; Freud, 1905/1947; Moore, 1945; Mowrer, 1953). There is reason to believe that these etiological hypotheses were based upon two clinical observations: That adult homosexual males reported more often than did heterosexual males that (a) in their childhood their father had been absent, or (b) that their childhood relationship with their father had been unsatisfactory. It is impossible, in practice, to test the hypothesis that physical or emotional removal of the father causes homosexuality. However, it is possible to test the clinical impression that there is a correlation between homosexuality and retrospective self-reports of father-absence or poor father-son relations.

Several studies have compared the relative frequency with which father-loss or absence is reported by heterosexual vs. homosexual samples; their outcomes have varied to a surprisingly high degree (Freund, Langevin, Zajac, Steiner, & Zajac, 1974; Freund & Pinkava, 1961; O'Connor, 1964; Terman & Miles, 1936; West, 1959). Obviously, such a comparison must take into account socioeconomic variables which might be related to frequency of father-desertion or other modes of family breakup, and has to be carried out on large, stratified and matched samples. The fact that none of the relevant studies has employed sophisticated sampling techniques might explain the lack of agreement in their findings.

Retrospective self-report of parental relationships. Various semicontrolled studies seemed to indicate that adult male homosexuals retrospectively report relatively poor childhood relationships with their fathers (Bieber, Dain, Dince, Drellich, Grand, Gundlach, Kremer, Rifkin, Wilbur, & Bieber, 1962; Bieber & Bieber, 1979; Jonas, 1944; Nash & Hayes, 1965; O'Connor, 1964; West, 1959), and the same is true of controlled studies (Bell, Weinberg, & Hammersmith, 1981; Bene, 1965; Freund & Pinkava, 1961; Siegelman, 1974, 1981). Siegelman (1974) demonstrated that the difference between heterosexual and homosexual males, in regard to retrospectively reported father-son relationships, disappears when both groups are represented by individuals who score low on neuroticism. Siegelman's finding suggests that this difference in retrospective reports is less likely to be related to a difference in the actual behavior of the fathers of homosexual sons than to some difference in homosexual boys' *response* to their fathers' behavior (or to systematic differences in adult homosexuals' memories of childhood). This tentative interpretation of Siegelman's finding would, in turn, seem to point toward the only well-established personality difference between heterosexuals and homosexuals, *viz.*, the difference in childhood gender identity.

Early observations of abnormally close mother-son relationships in the childhood of homosexuals (Fenichel, 1945; Freud, 1922/1953; p. 240; West, 1959) were not confirmed by Freund and Pinkava (1961) or Bene (1965), and the relatively greater closeness to the mother as compared to that to the father (Freund, Langevin, Zajac, Steiner, & Zajac, 1974) can be explained most plausibly by the unsatisfactory father-son relationship.

Cross gender identity. It has long been known that (nontranssexual) homosexual males and females are more likely than their heterosexual counterparts to produce retrospective accounts of cross gender behavior in childhood, and that they are more likely to exhibit cross gender behaviors and attitudes in adulthood as well. The early sexologists (Hirschfeld, 1914/1920; Krafft-Ebing, 1886/1890) pointed out various pertinent statements of their homosexual patients; in more recent times, masculinity-femininity scales have been employed to measure extent of cross gender identity in homosexuals.

The first masculinity-femininity scale was developed by Terman and Miles (1936); the best known examples are the Mf Scale of the MMPI (Hathaway & McKinley, 1943) and the Psychological Femininity Scale of the California Personality Inventory (Gough, 1952). The most recently devised scale (which is not unidimensional bipolar like the remainder) is the Bem Sex-Role Inventory (Bem, 1974), which measures femininity and masculinity separately. The items of Bem's scale are personality characteristics rated "as masculine or feminine on the basis of sex-typed social desirability" (p. 155) by male and female students. All the older masculinity-femininity scales were basically constructed by the authors themselves who selected sex-typed questionnaire items without regard to "desirability" and retained only those that were differentially answered by males and females.

In contrast to all the above-mentioned instruments, the Feminine Gender Identity (FGI) Scale for males (Freund, Nagler, Langevin, Zajac, & Steiner, 1974; Freund, Langevin, Satterberg, & Steiner, 1977), which was used in the present studies, was primarily constructed from self-report items identified by early sexologists as indicative of cross gender identity in homosexuals. Items in the FGI Scale were selected on the basis of their ability to discriminate among males, not on the basis of their ability to discriminate between males and females.

STUDY 1

Definitions. Prior to describing this study, definitions of certain age-sex preferences must be given. Heterosexual pedophilia is an erotic preference for female children under 11, and homosexual pedophilia is such a preference for male children. "Pure" hebephilia is an erotic preference for pubescents; because the onset of puberty comes somewhat later to males than to females, the most preferred age in homosexual hebephilia is a bit older. Thus, in heterosexual hebephilia, the preference is for 12 to 13 year old girls but may extend down as far as age 11 and as far up as 14 or 15. In homosexual hebephilia, the preferred age is somewhere between 11 and 16, but with the center of the range being somewhat higher than in heterosexual hebephilia. In pedohebephilia, the most preferred age spans an interval that belongs within the period of childhood but extends up to and including age 12, and sometimes 14 and possibly 15. Gynephilia is an erotic preference for physically mature females, and androphilia is such a preference for physically mature males.

Cross gender identity and preferred partner age. Freund, Scher, Chan, and Ben-Aron (1982), using the FGI Scale, compared the gender identity of seven groups of males: two samples of gynephiles (university students and incarcerates), two samples of androphiles (outpatients and nonpatient volunteers), a combined group of heterosexual pedophiles and pedohebephiles (hereafter, heterosexual pedo/pedohebephiles), a combined group of homosexual pedophiles and pedohebephiles (hereafter, homosexual pedo/pedohebephiles), and a group of "pure" homosexual hebephiles. The androphiles reported a greater degree of feminine gender identity than the gynephiles, the heterosexual pedo/pedohebephiles, or the homosexual pedo/pedohebephiles; there were no differences in gender identity among these latter groups. The degree of feminine gender identity reported by the homosexual hebephiles was intermediate between that reported by the androphiles, on the one hand, and that reported by the remaining groups, on the other.

The finding that homosexual pedo/pedohebephiles are similar in gender identity to gynephiles and heterosexual pedo/pedohebephiles rather than to androphiles suggests one possible approach to determining whether the emotional distance between fathers and homosexual sons relates to the sons' erotic preference for male partners or to the sons' atypical gender identity. If this distance relates to the erotic preference for male partners over female, then the father-son relationships of homosexual pedo/pedohebephiles should be similar to those of androphiles. If this distance relates to childhood gender identity, then the father-son relationships of homosexual pedo/pedohebephiles should be similar to those of gynephiles and heterosexual pedo/pedohebephiles. This was the question to which Study 1 was addressed.

Method

Subjects. There were four groups of subjects: Androphiles, gynephiles, a combined group of heterosexual pedophiles and pedohebephiles, and a combined group of homosexual pedophiles and pedohebephiles.

The pedo/pedohebephiles were patients of the Clarke Institute of Psychiatry. They were referred for assessment by their lawyers or by the courts, or had obtained a referral under pressure from their families or others. Only a small minority came complaining of a strong erotic attraction to minors, without any accusation as far as we knew. Included in the heterosexual pedo/pedohebephilic group were males accused of sexually approaching two or more female children, or two or more females younger than 15, including at least one prepubescent. Included in the homosexual pedo/pedohebephilic group were males accused of sexually approaching one or more male children or one or more 12 to 16 year old pubescent males. Those males who, without being accused, complained about strong erotic attraction to children and pubescents were included in the appropriate sex-age group. All pedo/pedohebephiles were excluded whose sexual approach consisted only of indecent exposure, whose interaction with minors had occurred only within their own families (incest cases), or who were more than 55 years old.

The gynephilic and androphilic samples were constructed so as to approximate the two pedo/pedohebephilic groups in regard to age, education, and sample size. The initial pool of males from which the androphilic sample was drawn consisted of androphilic men counseled at the Clarke Institute of Psychiatry. Most came with the request to be made heterosexual, or at least more bisexual. They came under pressure from a variety of sources, e.g., from their families, or from wives complaining about infrequency or lack of intercourse. Some were afraid that their friends and families would abandon them if they knew of their erotic preference. Others, particularly heterosexually married ones, had been caught having homosexual interactions in a public place; a few came because of erectile difficulties. None came primarily for a neurotic or psychotic disorder, and none reported an erotic interest in physically immature males. The formal psychometric criterion for inclusion in this group was a score of nine or higher on a 13-item "Andro" Scale, which measures erotic interest in physically mature males (see Freund, Steiner, & Chan, 1982, for further details). Verbally reported interest in females or actual heterosexual experience did not form any part of the criteria for inclusion in this group.

The initial subject pool, from which the gynephilic sample was drawn, consisted of paid volunteers recruited (and tested) at government employment offices. These males were screened for erotic interest in any type of partner other than physically mature females on the basis of their responses to 15 questionnaire items concerning erotic attraction to males and females of various ages. A subject was excluded at this stage if he responded in the anomalous direction to more than one item; 23 of 110 paid volunteers (21%) were eliminated according to this criterion.

All subjects were further screened for inclusion in one of the four diagnostic groups with a set of questionnaire items regarding the intactness of their family of origin. A subject was excluded if he had lived more than two years in an institution (orphanage, reform school, boarding school, and so on) prior to the age of 15, or if he had been raised in a home with no father or father-substitute prior to the age of 12. There was only one subject whose father or father-substitute was continuously present, while a mother or mother-substitute was absent for some interval prior to the age of 12; he was included in the analysis of father-son relations.

The total number of subjects in the four final groups was 194: 48 heterosexual pedo/pedohebephiles, mean age, 33.4 yrs (SD, 12.3 yrs); 50 gynephiles, mean age, 28.0 yrs (SD, 2.7 yrs); 56 homosexual pedo/pedohebephiles, mean age, 31.1 yrs (SD, 10.6 yrs); and 40 androphiles, mean age, 29.4 yrs (SD, 6.6 yrs). All four groups had similar mean educational levels, falling between 8 and 12 grades completed.

Materials. The dependent measures of parent-son relations were two

four-item mini-scales: the Father-Son Distance Scale and the Mother-Son Distance Scale (see Table 1). The reliabilities of these two measures had previously been established with a separate sample that consisted of 45 androphilic and 87 gynephilic volunteers, 36 androphilic

Table 1

The Father-Son Distance Scale with
Scoring Weights Given in Parentheses

1. Before about age 6, how do you remember feeling about your father (or if not present, other adult male who raised or helped raise you? If more than one, choose the one with whom you lived the longest during this period).

    a. liked him very much (1)
    b. liked him (2)
    c. neither liked nor disliked him (3)
    d. didn't like him very much (4)
    e. didn't like him at all (5)
    f. had no father or other male who helped raise you during this time, or spent most of this period in an institution, boarding school, etc. (exclude subject)
    g. unsure or don't remember (3)

2. Between the ages of about 6 and 12, how do you remember feeling about your father (or if not present, other adult male who helped raise you? If more than one, choose the one with whom you lived the longest during this period).

    a. liked him very much (1)
    b. liked him (2)
    c. neither liked nor disliked him (3)
    d. didn't like him very much (4)
    e. didn't like him at all (5)
    f. had no father or other adult male who helped raise you during this time, or spent most of this period in a public institution, boarding school, etc. (exclude subject)
    g. unsure or don't remember (3)

3. Up to about 6 years of age, how do you remember your father treating you (or if not present, other adult male who helped raise you)?

    a. very lovingly (1)
    b. lovingly (2)
    c. not very lovingly (3)
    d. with some dislike (4)
    e. had no father or other adult male who helped raise you during this time, or spent most of this period in a public institution, boarding school, etc. (exclude subject)

4. Between the ages of 6 and 12, how do you remember your father treating you (or if not present, other adult male who helped raise you)?

    a. very lovingly (1)
    b. lovingly (2)
    c. not very lovingly (3)
    d. with some dislike (4)
    e. had no father or other adult male who helped raise you during this time, or spent most of this period in a public institution, boarding school, etc. (exclude subject)

Note: The Mother-Son Distance Scale is identically scored and similarly worded, *mutatis mutandis*.

patients, 89 patients with a courtship disorder (voyeurism, exhibition-ism, toucheurism/frotteurism, and the preferential rape pattern) or erotic hyperdominance (borderline sadism), and 137 pedophiles and hebephiles. The alpha reliability of the Father-Son Distance Scale was .89, and that of the Mother-Son Distance Scale, .85. The eight items making up the two scales were embedded within the most recent version of the senior author's unpublished Erotic Preferences Examination Scheme (EPES), which also included the above-mentioned questionnaire items used for screening the subjects.

Results

A one-way analysis of variance carried out on the Father-Son scores of the four groups showed that there were significant differences among the group means, $F (3, 190) = 4.94$, $p = .0025$. A Duncan multiple range test carried out at the .05 level showed that the androphilic group retrospectively reported more distant relations with their fathers than any of the other three groups, which did not differ from one another. An analysis of variance performed on the Mother-Son scores revealed no significant differences among any of the groups, $F (3, 189) = 1.34$, $p = .26$.

Discussion

Study 1 showed that the androphiles, the only group among those compared known to exhibit a measurably greater degree of feminine gender identity, were also the only group to report significantly poorer father-son relations; the retrospectively reported father-son relationships of the homosexual pedo/pedohebephiles did not differ from those of the gynephiles or the heterosexual pedo/pedohebephiles. This outcome would appear to suggest that retrospective self-reports of adverse father-son relations have nothing to do with preferred partner sex (hetero-sexuality vs. homosexuality), but that they are connected with feminine gender identity.

There is, however, a weak point in the above argument: The andro-philic subjects were patients, and as already mentioned, Siegelman (1974, 1981) found that the androphilic-gynephilic difference in father-son relations disappears when both groups are represented by individuals low on neuroticism. One could reply to such an objection that the members of our androphilic patient group came for counselling in order to adjust to a heterosexual or homosexual lifestyle and not to be treated for a neurotic or psychotic disorder; the counterargument could, in turn, be made that non-neurotic androphiles would have adjusted with-out professional help.

There is a second, serious objection which might be raised to Study 1: Poor father-son relations might be associated specifically with the erotic preference for *physically mature* male partners. If this were the case, then our finding of normal father-son relations among the homosexual pedo/pedohebephiles would not rule out the possibility that the poor father-son relations of androphiles are connected to their erotic preference *per se* rather than to their childhood gender identity or behavior. This second objection would remain even if Study 1 were replicated with non-patient androphiles. Thus, it was necessary, in Studies 2 and 3, to move to a different experimental design, one which could provide evidence complementary to that of Study 1.

The lack of group differences in recalled mother-son relationships is not in agreement with early clinical reports but is consistent with the results of the systematic studies cited above. An earlier study (Freund, Langevin, Zajac, Steiner & Zajac, 1974) which has been interpreted as showing an androphilic-gynephilic difference in mother-son relations, actually involved relative preference for the mother vs. the father; a greater *relative* preference for the mother could, and probably did, reflect more negative feelings toward the father rather than greater closeness to the mother. West's (1959) seemingly positive finding of a difference in mother-son relations rests on evaluations by professionals who certainly knew the hypotheses of the earlier writers regarding mother-son closeness and androphilia. Of course, the possibility remains that future studies, using measures more subtle than ours, might show that androphiles are, as a group, closer in childhood to their mothers than gynephiles.

STUDY 2

The enormous variability in gender identity exhibited by androphilic males, both in their social presentation as adults and in their retrospective accounts of childhood gender role behavior, suggests a second strategy for approaching our central question. If the relatively poor father-son relations reported by androphiles are somehow connected to childhood gender identity, then those androphiles who report the greatest degree of cross gender behavior in childhood should also tend to be the ones to report the worst relationships with their fathers. If, on the other hand, childhood gender identity is quite irrelevant to poor father-son relationships, and such relationships are actually connected to the erotic preference for physically mature male partners *per se,* then no correlation between feminine gender identity and recalled father-son distance should be seen within the androphilic population.

Method

Subjects. Both the gynephilic and androphilic samples consisted of paid nonpatient volunteers, the latter recruited through homophile organizations. Two earlier investigations employing many of these same subjects have previously been reported (Freund, Langevin, Zajac, Steiner, & Zajac, 1974; Freund, Nagler, Langevin, Zajac & Steiner, 1974). Those two groups were screened for erotic interest in any type of partner other than physically mature females and males, respectively, on the basis of their responses to various questionnaire items concerning erotic attraction to males and females of different ages. Subjects were excluded whose questionnaire responses indicated that they had not been raised in completely intact nuclear families to the age of 12, as were subjects who failed to give a valid response to any questionnaire item used in the study.

The final number of subjects in the androphilic group was 147, and in the gynephilic group, 132. The mean age of the gynephiles was 27.6 yrs (SD = 9.4 yrs) and that of the androphiles, 27.4 yrs (SD = 7.6 yrs). In both groups, the modal educational level was university studies without graduation,with the second most frequent educational level being university graduation.

Materials. The present subjects completed the earliest version of the EPES. This questionnaire included the first (English) version of the FGI Scale for males (Freund, Nagler, Langevin, Zajac & Steiner, 1974). Only Part A of the scale was used in this study. One item was assigned scoring weights slightly different from the published weights, giving a possible total score of 25 rather than 24. The Father-Son and Mother-Son Distance Scales contained in the first version of the EPES differed slightly from the same scales in the later versions (Table 1), having fewer response options to the first two items; all items had a maximum score of "4."

Results

The two groups were compared with regard to the following demographic and family background variables: the age of both parents when the subject was born, educational level of both parents, alcohol use by both parents in the two years before the subject was born, and whether "someone" (no further identity was specified in the questionnaire item) who brought the subject up was drunk at least once a week. The only significant difference was on the last item mentioned, with 6% of gynephiles vs. 14% of androphiles responding "yes" rather than "no, not sure, or can't remember" ($p < .05$, two-tailed).

The androphiles reported more distant relationships with their fathers, $r = .38$, $p < .001$ (one-tailed). There was no significant correlation between erotic partner preference and mother-son distance. There was a high correlation between androphilia and feminine gender identity, $r =$ .59, $p < .001$ (one-tailed); however, this last finding should not be regarded as a replication, since it was based on much the same data already reported by Freund, Nagler, Langevin, Zajac & Steiner, (1974). These three correlations were virtually unaffected by partialling out whether "someone" who brought the subject up was drunk once a week, by partialling out all demographic and family variables simultaneously, or by partialling out any of a great number of subsets of demographic and family variables also investigated.

The correlation between father-son distance and feminine gender identity and the correlation between mother-son distance and feminine gender identity were computed separately for the androphiles and the gynephiles. For the gynephilic group, neither correlation was significant. Among the androphiles, there was also no correlation between gender identity and mother-son distance, but there was a significant correlation between feminine gender identity and father-son distance, $r =$ .21, $p = .005$ (one-tailed). The four regression lines corresponding to the above correlations are plotted in Figure 1. This figure shows that, as feminine gender identity increases, so does the self-reported distance between an androphilic son and his father.

Within the androphilic group, partialling out mother-son distance slightly increased the correlation between father-son distance and feminine gender identity, from .21 to .24 ($p = .002$, one-tailed). Carrying out this same operation within the gynephilic group produced essentially no change.

Among the gynephiles, the correlation between the Mother-Son scores and Father-Son scores was .47, $p < .001$, two-tailed. Among the androphiles, this correlation was also positive and significant, although smaller, $r = .21$, $p < .02$, two-tailed.

The variable, whether "someone" who brought the subject up was drunk once a week (scored "yes" $= 1$, "no, not sure, or can't remember" $= 0$), was significantly and positively correlated with father-son distance as well as mother-son distance within both groups, but was not significantly correlated with feminine gender identity within either group. Within the androphilic group, partialling the alcohol-abuse variable out of the correlation between father-son distance and feminine gender identity increased that correlation slightly, from .21 to .23 ($p = .003$, one-tailed).

Discussion

The results of Study 2 confirmed our prediction, based in part upon the results of Study 1, that among androphilic males feminine gender identity and retrospective reports of poor father-son relations are positively correlated. However, although the correlation obtained was sta-

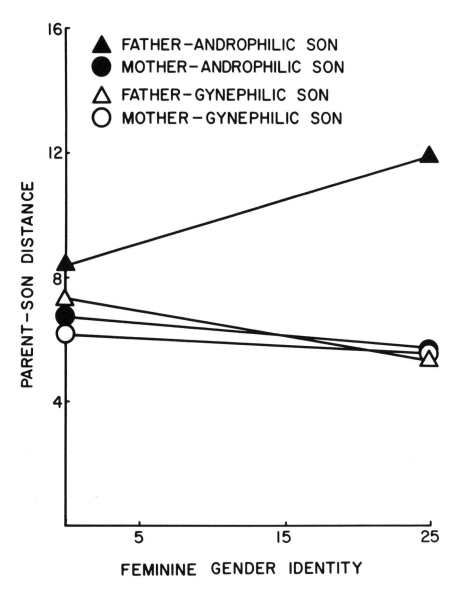

FIGURE 1. Regression lines relating the FGI raw scores of androphilic and gynephilic subjects to Mother-Son Distance and Father-Son Distance raw scores. The ordinate is read as "Father-Son Distance" for regression lines marked with a triangle, and as "Mother-Son Distance" for regression lines marked with a circle. Higher FGI scores indicate more feminine gender identity; higher Mother-Son and Father-Son scores indicate more remote (or more hostile) mother-son or father-son relationships.

tistically significant, its size was not as large as one would expect if feminine gender identity played a decisive role in such self-reports. The explanation that seems most likely in the present context is that this correlation is an underestimate, caused by the shortcomings of our psychometric devices, particularly those of our mini-scale for the retrospective assessment of father-son relations.

A positive correlation between feminine gender identity and poor father-son relations (retrospectively reported) has previously been observed by Nash and Hayes (1965). Unlike the present authors, they included homosexual hebephiles as well as androphiles in their sample. Nash and Hayes categorized their subjects as "actives, active-passives, and passives," and found that the "actives" tended to report better father-son relations than the "passives."

The lack of any correlation within the androphilic group between feminine gender identity and retrospectively reported mother-son relationships was to be expected, since Study 1 had already demonstrated that the mother-son scores of the androphiles did not differ from those of the other subjects. On the other hand, their gender identity and father distance scores had shown, relative to the mean scores of the other three groups, a parallel displacement. The lack of any correlation within the gynephilic group between feminine gender identity and retrospectively reported father-son relationships was also predictable; there is no reason to believe that feminine gender identity is a meaningful dimension in gynephiles, with the exception of transvestites; heterosexual male-to-female transsexuals; and intermediate types (Freund, Steiner & Chan, 1982). This point was empirically demonstrated in an unpublished study by the present second author, who analyzed the scores of 193 nontransvestite, nontranssexual gynephiles on Part A of the extended (i.e., 1977) FGI Scale. The strongest factor to emerge from a factor analysis of these data accounted for only 9.6% of the total variance, and the alpha reliability of the scale, computed from this all-gynephilic sample, was only .53.

STUDY 3

The results of Study 1 were consistent with the hypothesis that the emotional distance between fathers and androphilic sons is related to the sons' atypical gender identity (or observable gender role behavior) rather than to the sons' erotic preference for males. However, more direct evidence of this view was Study 2's finding that those androphiles who reported the greatest degree of cross gender behavior in childhood also tended to report the worst relationships with their fathers. Therefore, it was important to replicate the latter finding, particularly since the size of the correlation obtained in Study 2 was rather small. We also considered it desirable to extend the generality of this result by demonstrating that this correlation obtains among androphilic patients as well as androphilic nonpatients.

Method

Subjects. These were androphilic males counselled at the Clarke Institute of Psychiatry, including those 40 whose data were used in Study 1. The problems that led these men to seek counselling, as well as the criteria used for including a subject in this group, have already been described in that study. Subjects were excluded who had lived more than two years in an institution prior to the age of 15, who had not been raised by both a mother (or substitute) and father (or substitute) until the age of 12, or who lacked a valid response to any questionnaire item used in the study. The 89 remaining subjects had a mean age of 27.9 yrs (SD, 8.0 yrs); their modal educational level was high school graduation, with approximately equal numbers of subjects reporting higher and lower levels of educational achievement.

Materials. These subjects completed the most recent version of the EPES, which includes the versions of the Father-Son and Mother-Son Scales presented in Table 1 as well as Parts A, B, and C of the *extended* Feminine Gender Identity (FGI) Scale for males (Freund et al., 1977). Part A of the FGI Scale contains most of the items pertaining to childhood and early adolescence. (Additional construct validation of this part of the Scale has been provided by Blanchard, McConkey, Roper, & Steiner, in press.) The scoring weights used for all parts of the FGI Scale were identical to the published weights (Freund et al., 1977).

Results

The correlation between Part A of the FGI Scale and distant father-son relations was .18, which was statistically significant ($p = .05$, one-tailed). When the mother-son score was partialled out, this correlation increased marginally, to .20 ($p = .03$, one-tailed). Father-son distance did not correlate with Parts B or C of the Scale, and mother-son distance did not correlate with any part of the Scale. As in Study 2, there was a significant positive correlation between Mother-Son scores and Father-Son scores, $r = .38$, $p < .001$, two-tailed.

The variable, whether "someone" who brought the subject up was drunk once a week (scored as in Study 2), was positively correlated with father-son distance ($r = .24$; $p < .02$, one-tailed) but was not significantly correlated with mother-son distance or with Part A of the

FGI Scale. Partialling the alcohol-abuse variable out of the correlation between father-son distance and Part A of the FGI Scale increased that correlation slightly, from .18 to .21 ($p < .03$, one-tailed).

Discussion

The results of Study 3 replicated those of Study 2 quite closely. The size of the correlations between father-son distance and childhood gender identity, as measured by Part A of the FGI Scale, was similar in the two studies; the finding that retrospective reports of father-son relations prior to the age of 12 did not correlate with Parts B or C of the FGI Scale can probably be explained by the fact that most of the items they contain concern adult feelings and behavior.

The correlation between father-son distance and mother-son distance was somewhat larger in Study 3 than it had been for the androphiles in Study 2. This correlation, which is mainly of passing interest, indicates that self-reports of good father-son relations tend to be found in association with self-reports of good mother-son relations.

GENERAL DISCUSSION

The central topic of the three present studies was the interconnection of feminine gender identity (in males), erotically preferred partner sex, and retrospectively reported father-son distance. Study 1 compared the retrospectively reported father-son relationships of gynephiles, androphiles, heterosexual pedophiles (including pedohebephiles), and homosexual pedophiles (including pedohebephiles). The androphiles were the only group to report significantly poorer father-son relations. Because a previous study of these four types of males (Freund, Scher, Chan & Ben-Aron, 1982) showed that feminine gender identity occurs more than exceptionally only among androphiles, the result of Study 1 was interpreted as suggesting that not homosexuality *per se* but much more likely feminine gender identity is the true correlate of indifferent or antagonistic father-son relations. Studies 2 and 3 confirmed Study 1's suggestion of such an association by demonstrating that, within the androphilic population, those individuals who reported the greatest degree of cross gender behavior in childhood also tended to report the worst relationships with their fathers.

The finding that, among androphiles, retrospective reports of father-son distance are positively correlated with reports of feminine (or insufficiently masculine) gender identity in childhood does not, by itself, rule out the possibility that there is also a sizeable direct correlation between androphilia and father-son estrangement. However, the convergence of the regression lines at the y-intercept in Figure 1 strongly suggests that, at a gender identity score of zero or near zero, there would be no difference in the father-son relationships of androphiles and gynephiles. The cleanest experimental test of the hypothesis that childhood gender identity does *not* completely account for the andro-philic-gynephilic difference in father-son distance would involve a dem-onstration that the father-son distance scores of gynephilic controls are still lower than those of a large group of androphiles who have zero or near zero feminine gender identity scores. This very costly test of a possibility, which has already been made quite unlikely, has not been carried out.

The observation that adult androphiles tend to recall poorer childhood relations with their fathers than gynephiles has usually been interpreted by psychoanalytically oriented authors as evidence that a father's in-difference or hostility toward a son may lead to the son's becoming homosexual (see citations in the Introduction). In contrast, Hirschfeld (1914/1920) suggested that the poor father-son relationship may result from the father's reaction to the homosexual son's femininity. Such causal interpretations of the correlations in the retrospective data are arbitrary. Better insight can be obtained by concurrent investigations of the family situation of effeminate boys, many of whom later turn out to be homosexual (Green, 1979; Money & Russo, 1979; Zuger, 1978). This method was emloyed by Zuger (1980), who interviewed the parents of effeminate boys who were his patients. Zuger's data, which are purely clinical and anecdotal, strongly indicate that the characteristic father-son and mother-son relationships retrospectively reported by adult androphiles do correspond to the real situation in the childhood of feminine boys. Zuger found that increased father-son distance was in-duced by the feminine boys themselves. This finding does not, however, rule out the possibility that the father's negative reaction to the son's femininity may also contribute to their estrangement, as suggested by Hirschfeld.

In the present investigation, there was no difference between the retrospectively reported mother-son relations of the androphiles and those of the other groups examined. This might be due to the crudeness of our Mother-Son mini-scale. However, the present result together with those of previous studies (Bene, 1965; Freund & Pinkava, 1961) makes it very likely that, if there is an androphilic-gynephilic difference in mother-son relations, it is much smaller than the difference in father-son relations.

Our instruments for measuring father-son distance and feminine gen-der identity were adequate to enable us to demonstrate that, among androphiles, some correlation between these phenomena does exist, but these instruments cannot be regarded as sophisticated enough to estimate the magnitude of this association. The grossly exploratory nature of the Mother-Son and Father-Son Distance mini-scales is evident in their extreme brevity and in the lack of variety in the items. The reason why the FGI Scale might not be optimal for the magnitude-estimation task mentioned above is less obvious: This scale was constructed by selecting individual items that discriminate between androphiles and gynephiles. The set of items selected by following this procedure will not necessarily be identical to that set which would discriminate maximally within all-androphilic samples. Thus any quantitative estimate of the degree to which androphilic gender identity and androphilic father-son distance are correlated must await the selection or development of more sophisticated parent-son relationship measures, and the development of a gender identity scale that allows the greatest possible discrimination among androphiles. The latter task would involve selecting items according to the intercorrelations of the responses of androphilic subjects only—an undertaking requiring at least a few hundred subjects screened for age-of-partner as well as sex-of-partner preference.

A secondary finding in Study 2 was that androphiles reported more frequently than gynephiles that some adult *in loco parentis* had been drunk at least once a week; our experience in administering the EPES to a great number of patients of various diagnostic categories, who were contemporaneously interviewed, has been that a positive answer almost invariably refers to the examinee's father or father-substitute. When Freund and Pinkava (1961) first observed the differential frequency with which androphiles and gynephiles retrospectively reported father-drunkenness, they pointed out the possibility that this difference might just reflect a tendency for androphiles, who like their fathers less, to be less tolerant in evaluating their fathers' behavior.

In the present investigation, a significant correlation was found between poor father-son relations and reports of (what we may assume to be) father's drunkenness, in both gynephilic and androphilic samples. No association was found, in androphilic males, between feminine gender identity and reports of father's drunkenness. This pattern of results is susceptible to two interpretations. Let us assume first that the androphilic-gynephilic difference in such reports does not so much reflect reality as a bias in the androphilic son's attitude toward the father, i.e., that the androphiles' increased recollection of father-drunkenness is merely a function of greater animosity. In this case, the lack of correlation between feminine gender identity and reports of father-drunkenness suggests some component in androphiles' heightened animosity toward their fathers that does not vary in proportion to childhood femininity and which may have some other origin. Alternatively, let us assume that the subjects' reports of father-drunkenness are realistic; this would imply that androphiles are actually more likely to have fathers who abused alcohol. Our data would not, however, support the further interpretation that alcohol abuse might have some direct biological effect upon the probability of homosexual offspring; there was no difference in the frequency with which androphiles and gynephiles reported that their fathers or their mothers had abused alcohol in the two years before the subject was born. In any event, the gynephilic-androphilic difference in retrospectively reported paternal alcohol abuse would have to be replicated with socioeconomically matched samples before any follow-up of this result would be possible.

REFERENCES

Allen, C. *The sexual perversions and abnormalities.* London: Oxford University Press, 1940.
Allen, C. The problems of homosexuality. *International Journal of Sexology,* 1952, *6*, 40-42.
Allen, C. *Homosexuality.* London: Staples Press, 1958.
Allen, C. *A textbook of psychosexual disorders.* London: Oxford University Press, 1962.
Bell, A. P., Weinberg, M. S., & Hammersmith, S. K. *Sexual preference: Its development in men and women.* Bloomington: Indiana University Press, 1981.
Bem, S. L. The measurement of psychological androgyny. *Journal of Consulting and Clinical Psychology,* 1974, *42*, 155-162.
Bene, E. On the genesis of male homosexuality: An attempt at clarifying the role of the parents. *British Journal of Psychiatry,* 1965, *111*, 803-813.
Bieber, I., & Bieber, T. B. Male homosexuality. *Canadian Journal of Psychiatry,* 1979, *24*, 409-421.
Bieber, I., Dain, H. J., Dince, P. R., Drellich, M. G., Grand, R. H., Kremer, M. W., Rifkin, A. H., Wilbur, C. B., & Bieber, T. B. *Homosexuality: A psychoanalytic study.* New York: Vintage Books, 1962.
Blanchard, R., McConkey, J. G., Roper, V., & Steiner, B. W. Measuring physical aggressiveness in heterosexual, homosexual, and transsexual males. *Archives of Sexual Behavior,* in press.
Fenichel, O. *The psychoanalytic theory of neurosis.* New York: W. W. Norton, 1945.
Ferenczi, S. The nosology of male homosexuality. In H. M. Ruitenbeek (Ed.), *The problem of homosexuality in modern society.* New York: Dutton, 1963. (Originally published, 1914.)
Freud, S. *Drei Abhandlungen zur Sexualtheorie.* Wien: Franz Deuticke, 1947. (Originally published, 1905.)
Freud, S. [Certain neurotic mechanisms in jealousy, paranoia and homosexuality.] *Collected papers* (Vol. 2). London: Hogarth Press, 1953. (Originally published, 1922.)
Freud, K., Langevin, R., Satterberg, J., & Steiner, B. W. Extension of the gender identity scale for males. *Archives of Sexual Behavior,* 1977, *6*, 507-519.
Freud, K., Langevin, R., Zajac, Y., Steiner, B. W., & Zajac, A. Parent-child relations in transsexual and non-transsexual homosexual males. *British Journal of Psychiatry,* 1974, *124*, 22-23.
Freud, K., Nagler, E., Langevin, R., Zajac, A., & Steiner, B. W. Measuring feminine gender identity in homosexual males. *Archives of Sexual Behavior,* 1974, *3*, 249-260.
Freud, K., & Pinkava, V. Homosexuality in man and its association with parental relationships. *Review of Czechoslovak Medicine,* 1961, *7*, 32-40.
Freud, K., Scher, H., Chan, S., & Ben-Aron, M. Experimental analysis of pedophilia. *Behaviour Research and Therapy,* 1982, *20*, 105-112.
Freud, K., Steiner, B. W., & Chan, S. Two types of cross gender identity. *Archives of Sexual Behavior,* 1982, *11*, 49-63.
Gough, H. G. Identifying psychological femininity. *Educational and Psychological measurement,* 1952, *17*, 427-439.
Green, R. Childhood cross-gender behavior and subsequent sexual preference. *American Journal of Psychiatry,* 1979, *136*, 106-108.

Hathaway, S. R., and McKinley, J. C. *The Minnesota Multiphasic Personality Inventory.* New York: University of Minnesota Press, 1943.

Hirschfeld, M. *Die Homosexualität des Mannes und des Weibes* (2nd ed.). Berlin: L. Marcus, 1920. (Originally published, 1914.)

Jonas, C. H. An objective approach to the personality and environment in homosexuality. *Psychiatric Quarterly,* 1944, *18,* 626-641.

Krafft-Ebing, R. *Psychopathia Sexualis.* Stuttgart: F. Enke, 1890. (Originally published, 1886.)

Money, J., & Russo, A. J. Homosexual outcome of discordant gender identity/role in childhood: Longitudinal follow-up. *Journal of Pediatric Psychology,* 1979, *4,* 29-41.

Moore, T. V. The pathogenesis and treatment of homosexual disorders. *Journal of Personality,* 1945, *14,* 47-83.

Mowrer, O. H. *Psychotherapy: Theory and research.* New York: Ronald Press, 1953.

Nash, J., & Hayes, F. The parental relationships of male homosexuals: Some theoretical issues and a pilot study. *Australian Journal of Psychology,* 1965, *17,* 35-43.

O'Connor, P. J. Aetiological factors in homosexuality as seen in Royal Air Force psychiatric practice. *British Journal of Psychiatry,* 1964, *110,* 381-391.

Siegelman, M. Parental background of male homosexuals and heterosexuals. *Archives of Sexual Behavior,* 1974, *3,* 3-18.

Siegelman, M. Parental backgrounds of homosexual and heterosexual men: A cross national replication. *Archives of Sexual Behavior,* 1981, *10,* 505-513.

Terman, L. M., & Miles, C. *Sex and personality: Studies in masculinity and femininity.* New York: McGraw-Hill, 1936.

West, D. J. Parental figures in the genesis of male homosexuality. *International Journal of Social Psychiatry,* 1959, *5,* 85-97.

Zuger, B. Effeminate behavior present in boys from childhood: Ten additional years of follow-up. *Comprehensive Psychiatry,* 1978, *19,* 363-369.

Zuger, B. Homosexuality and parental guilt. *British Journal of Psychiatry,* 1980, *137,* 55-57.

Femininity, Masculinity, and Sexual Orientation: Some Cross-Cultural Comparisons

Michael W. Ross, PhD

The Flinders University of South Australia Medical School

ABSTRACT. Predominantly homosexual males from Australia (n = 163), Sweden (n = 176) and Finland (n = 149) were compared on the Bem Sex-Role Inventory and on various measures of partner preference in order to establish the relationship between degree of homosexuality in terms of Kinsey Scale position and gender identity. Results suggest that while there is no relationship between femininity and degree of homosexuality, masculinity is inversely related depending on the degree of sex role stereotyping and anti-homosexual attitudes of the society the subjects live in. Such findings suggest that deviant gender identity is a function not of homosexuality as such but of societal attitudes which may reinforce a homosexual role.

The issue of the relationship among sexual orientation, femininity, and masculinity is not a new one. Freud (1922/1955) indicated that homosexual orientation may arise from the over-identification of a male individual with his mother. This view has gained considerable credence. Perhaps the most explicit and testable model of the relationship between sex role and sexual orientation has been put forward by Money (1974; 1977). In this model, incongruity of gender identity, "the private experience of sex role" (Money & Ehrhardt, 1972), is equated with the individual's form of sexual expression. Thus, transsexuals are believed to prefer a same-sex partner, identifying so much with the opposite sex that they wish to change to that sex in role and anatomy. Homosexuals are believed to prefer same-sex partners, identifying with, but not wishing to change to, the opposite sex. Money (1977) has narrowed the application of his position to only effeminate male and masculine female homosexuals. Transvestism and bisexuality are seen by Money as episodic variations, implying that there is less inappropriate (i.e., less opposite-sex) gender identity in these individuals. Money, however,

Dr. Ross is in the Department of Psychiatry, The Flinders University of South Australia Medical School, Bedford Park 5042, South Australia. Requests for reprints should be sent to him at that address.

© 1983 by The Haworth Press, Inc. All rights reserved.

does not make clear whether he believes transvestism and bisexuality to be instances of a less strong opposite-sex gender identity, although this is implied in his schema (see Table 1).

Older approaches to sexual behavior, such as that of Kinsey, Pomeroy and Martin (1948), have placed sexual behavior from exclusive homosexuality to exclusive heterosexuality on a single continuum. In terms of sexual preference, however, Shively and DeCecco (1977) have indicated that sex role and sexual orientation could also be considered separate continua. Nevertheless, in both the Money and Kinsey conceptualizations, bisexuality is seen as a mode of sexual expression incorporating a lesser degree of inappropriate gender role than exclusive homosexuality.

This approach has been questioned by Ross, Rogers, and McCullough (1978). They suggest that the linking of sex role and homosexuality is, to some degree, a function of societal expectations. Where society is both highly sex-role differentiated and antihomosexual, people who wish to relate sexually with a member of the same sex may feel they must contain some attributes of, or may consider themselves to be partly, members of the opposite sex. In situations where both homophobia and strong sex differentiation are less intense, Ross et al. have shown that the degree of opposite-sex identification in homosexual men, using unicontinual (Ross, 1975) or bicontinual scales (Heilbrun & Thompson, 1977), is correspondingly reduced.

The conflicting theories of Money and Ross can be empirically tested in a variety of ways. First, if homosexuality and female sex role identity are linked in males, then feminine identity would be expected to decrease and masculine identity to increase as individuals classified themselves as less homosexual and more bisexual or heterosexual. Second, these differences would be expected to become more marked in a more antihomosexual and more rigidly sex-role differentiating society. At a third level, one might expect that the more opposite-sex gender identity

TABLE 1

TRANSPOSITIONS OF GENDER IDENTITY/ROLE

(From Money, 1974)

Degree of Transposition	Chronic	Episodic	Elective
Total	Transsexualism	Transvestism	Occupation
Partial	Obligative Homosexuality	Bisexualism	Recreation

was present in an individual, the more extreme and complementary they might expect a partner to be. Wilson and Nias (1976) report that individuals tend to seek complementarity rather than similarity of characteristics in partners. Thus, a bisexual in a homosexual encounter might prefer a fairly masculine partner, whereas an exclusively homosexual male may prefer a much more feminine individual.

What is being suggested here is a mirror-image of gender identity scale in partner preference. While the presence or absence of such a scale would not be conclusive evidence for either of the opposing arguments, it would throw some light on the nature of the continuum of sexual orientation and, in addition, confirm or negate the findings regarding the relationship between degree of inappropriate sex role and degree of homosexuality. The relationships between gender identity (as measured by social sex-role) and degree of homosexuality essentially describe the "homosexual role" in Western society (McIntosh, 1968).

Two major hypotheses may therefore be put forward. First, that there will be no significant relationship between position on the Kinsey continuum and sex-role identification as masculine or feminine, as measured by the Bem Sex-Role Inventory (Bem, 1974) and by semantic differential scales, in homosexual men. (Gender identity is here regarded as the intervening variable underlying social sex roles.) However, it is predicted that there will be significant differences in sex-role identification, using the same measures, between homosexual men drawn from a society in which there are stronger antihomosexual attitudes and greater sex-role differentiation (Australia) compared with ones in which both are weaker (Sweden and Finland). Finally, that semantic differential measures of masculinity and femininity of sexual partners will not be significantly related to degree of homosexuality (as measured on the Kinsey scale).

Respondents from Sweden, Finland, and Australia were chosen for several reasons. Chief among these was that all three are industrial and affluent Western societies of roughly similar size: Sweden had a population of 9 million, Australia of 13 million and Finland of 4 million. The Australia sample was selected from two east coast States: Queensland, with a population of 2½ million and Victoria, 3½ million. The other reason for selecting these three nations was their contrasting attitudes toward homosexuality, sex roles, and the status of the female. Sweden is both accepting of homosexuality (the laws proscribing it were removed in 1944) and has strong legislative support for equality between males and females. Finland has a similar attitude toward equality between the sexes, but it is more antihomosexual. Although homosexual acts between consenting adults are legal, it is legal to talk about homosexuality only in a negative way. In both Victoria and Queensland, at the time of data collection, homosexual acts were criminal and there was little legislation dealing with equality between the sexes. In fact, one writer (McKenzie, 1962) has commented that women in Australia have a less significant role in the professions and in public life and encounter more formal and informal discrimination than in any other industrial democracy.

Sweden and Australia were selected in order to match characteristics of respondents. Both are technologically advanced Western societies, both have high standards of living and are of roughly equal population. In terms of socio-political similarity, Banks and Gregg (1965) calculated their similarity, expressed as a correlation across the most important political factor they extracted, as .918 (Sweden) and .917 (Australia). In terms of the correlation of loadings across factors on a questionnaire of socio-political attitudes, Sidanius, Ekehammer and Ross (1979) found the attitudinal similarity between the two countries to be .972. Given these differences, it is possible to test, to a limited degree, the hypothesis that the social environment of homosexual men will affect gender identity and its relationship to degree of homosexuality.

METHOD

Sample

The samples were collected in 1977 and 1978 and consisted of 176 Swedish, 163 Australian, and 149 Finnish homosexual men. All three groups were presented with the research questionnaire translated into the appropriate language (Swedish or Finnish). The foreign language questionnaires were translated back into English by a second individual to check accuracy. The questionnaires were mailed with the newsletters of the major (or only) homosexual social rights organization in four cities: Stockholm, with a population of 1 million; Helsinki, 1/2 million; Melbourne, 3 million; and Brisbane, 1 million. In each case the organization also functioned as the main regional organization. Return rates were 44% for Sweden, 46.6% for Australia, and 54% for Finland. These percentages are based on the number of questionnaires given to the clubs to mail, which was equivalent to the number of males on their mailing lists. In all cases, the organizational aims of the clubs appeared identical. Sample characteristics appear in Table 2.

Given the large size of the sample, the lack of significance differences suggests that respondents were fairly well matched. The only significant differences were on the variables Religion and Social Class of Parents. The differences in degree of religious interest can be explained by the fact that some of the Australian sample were contacted through the Metropolitan Community Church, a Christian church with a predomi-

Table 2

Sample Characteristics

Variables	Sweden		Australia		Finland	
	M	SD	M	SD	M	SD
Age	30.9	7.4	31.9	11.4	28.4	7.8
Years Education	12.7	5.3	13.3	3.6	13.2	4.4
Kinsey Scale Position	6.6	0.8	6.7	1.0	6.5	0.9
Age When Actively Homosexual	20.8	7.4	19.3	12.1	20.4	7.2
Age Realised Homosexual	14.1	5.7	12.5	7.0	13.9	5.4
	n		n		n	
Religion[a] = Practising	11		52		10	
Nominal	91		51		66	
None	62		49		64	
Social Class [b] = Upper	32		8		4	
Middle	80		89		66	
Working	57		56		74	

a. $\chi^2(4) = 59.1$**

b. $\chi^2(4) = 35.3$**

* $p < .05$

** $p < .01$

nantly homosexual membership. There is no equivalent in Sweden or Finland. The higher proportion of Swedes who reported upper-class parents is difficult to explain, although it may be that Sweden has a much stronger aristocratic tradition than the other two countries. However, were these differences genuine, it would be expected that there would also be educational differences among the samples. There were, however, no significant differences between the samples (based on multiple t-tests) on age, education, position on the Kinsey Scale, age at which respondents realized they were homosexual, or age at which they became homosexually active.

Questionnaire

The questionnaire, which was part of a wider study on homosexuality in the three cultures, contained the Bem Sex-Role Inventory (BSRI), the Kinsey scale, and 5-point semantic differential scales. The semantic differential scales contained poles labeled "masculine" and "feminine" for indicating responses to two questions: (1) "How would you describe yourself when you first came out?"; (2) "How would you describe yourself now?". Similar semantic differentials, with the poles defined by the adjective pairs "masculine vs. feminine," "active vs. passive," and "rugged vs. delicate," were provided for responses to this question: "What characteristics do you prefer in a sexual partner?" The Chi-square test was used for analyzing ordinal data. Interval data were analyzed by multiple t-tests between samples. In the case of masculinity and femininity scores on the BSRI, linear regression coefficients were computed on the dependent variable of Kinsey Scale position.

RESULTS

Results are presented in Table 3 and Figure 1.

DISCUSSION

The results support the first hypothesis, that there would be no significant difference in position on the Kinsey Scale, for homosexuals in Sweden but not for those in Australia. In Sweden, neither masculinity nor femininity as measured by the BSRI was associated with degree of homosexuality. In Australia, masculinity (but not femininity) was significantly related to position on the Kinsey Scale, with the more homosexual individuals being the least masculine (Table 3). Interestingly, the relationship of masculinity with Kinsey Scale in the Finns, while not statistically significant, tended to be in the same direction.

Thus Money's (1974) contention that homosexuality and gender identity are interrelated would appear to be confirmed in the case of Australian homosexual men, but not for those in Sweden and Finland. Interpretation of this can be made in the light of the suggestion of Ross et al. (1978) that with greater antihomosexual legal and social attitudes, and with more rigid sex-role differentiation, more homosexual males will define themselves as feminine. In Sweden, with a much lesser degree of sex-role rigidity and antihomosexual attitudes, there is no significant relationship between masculinity and femininity on the one hand, and degree of homosexuality on the other.

Table 3

Correlations Between Semantic Differentials & the BSRI with Kinsey Scale Position

Semantic Differential & BSRI	Sweden	Australia	Finland
Masculine-Feminine [a] (when first came out)	.03	.16*	.13
Masculine-Feminine (now, self-assessment)	-.03	.09	-.04
Preferred Partners, Active-Passive	.01	.11	-.17*
Preferred Partners, Masculine-Feminine	-.17*	.11	-.00
Preferred Partners, Rugged-Delicate	.01	.09	-.04
BSRI Masculinity	-.03	-.18*	-.08
BSRI Femininity	-.01	-.01	-.01

a The right-hand term defines the high-scoring pole

* p< .05

The relationship between the three cultures in terms of masculinity is illustrated in Figure 1, where regression lines show the increase in slope as the society becomes more antihomosexual and sex-role rigid. Interestingly, femininity appears not to be related to degree of homosexuality in any of the three samples. Thus it would appear that Money (1974) is correct in ascribing a relationship between gender identity and degree of homosexuality, but only in societies that are antihomosexual and have relatively rigid sex roles. This suggests that the relationship between degree of homosexuality and gender identity is a socially based one rather than biologically inherent in a homosexual orientation.

The second hypothesis suggested that, using semantic differential scales for self-assessment of masculinity and femininity on a single scale, there would also be no significant differences between degree of homosexuality and sex role. Again, in Table 3, it can be seen that the relationship holds only for Australian homosexual men who rate themselves as less masculine as they rate themselves more homosexual

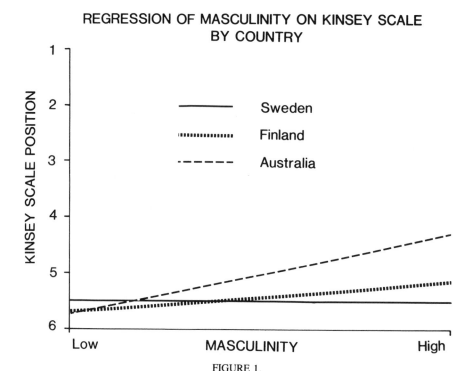

FIGURE 1.

when they first came out. This pattern fades over time, but there is still a negative relationship between masculinity and degree of homosexuality. While correlations for both Swedes and Finns were negative when they first came out as homosexual, the sign reverses for their assessment of their present level of masculinity. This interestingly suggests that in the more antihomosexual and sex-role rigid societies, there is a tendency for individuals to classify themselves as less masculine when they first come out, but for this self-ascription of the conventional homosexual role to drop off over time. The exception occurs in the most sex-role rigid society, Australia, where there was only a slight drop in correlation, but still in the direction of homosexual individuals assessing themselves as less masculine. In the other two cultures, there was no relationship between sex role and degree of homosexuality.

With regard to the femininity or masculinity of partners, the results are less clear. In general it can be seen that there are no significant correlations between position on the Kinsey scale and partner preferences, thus supporting the hypothesis that sex role is unrelated to degree of homosexuality. This hypothesis provides a test of Freudian theory that (1) male homosexuals will prefer as a sexual partner, "a girl with a penis" (Fisher & Greenberg, 1977); and (2) that there is a relationship between partner characteristics and sex role.

Directionality of the hypothesis, should significant results be achieved, would be more difficult to explain, since it could be postulated that individuals may choose partners unlike themselves (the complementarity option) or like themselves (the similarity option), thus leading to significant positive and negative correlations respectively. However, Wilson and Nias (1976) have indicated that most individuals choose similar partners, so this direction was selected in analyzing the data. Significant results indicate that Swedes would choose a more masculine partner the more homosexual they are, and that Finns would choose a more active partner the more homosexual they are. This does not support Freudian theory with regard to partner selection since homosexual men appear to prefer non-feminine attributes in male partners, while more heterosexual men appear to favor more feminine attributes. It is particularly interesting to note that with the Australians, the signs were reversed, again supporting the hypothesis that the association of high degree of homosexuality is associated with a high degree of femininity in terms of partner preference.

In conclusion, it is apparent that the relationship between degree of homosexuality and sex role is dependent not on homosexuality as such but on the attitudes toward homosexuality and sex-role rigidity in the society in which the homosexual lives. Thus Money's (1974) theory would appear to be correct for Australian homosexuals where sex roles are most rigid and laws most antihomosexual of the three countries compared. It is less correct for Finland, where sex roles are more liberal but laws tend to be somewhat antihomosexual; and incorrect for Sweden, where sex roles are again more liberal than in Australia and where homosexuals are guaranteed legal equality. Bearing in mind the difficulties of cross-cultural research and the impossibility of manipulation of independent variables, it can be tentatively suggested that any association of homosexuality and opposite-sex role identification is socially mediated. Such a finding does suggest that the homosexual role (Goode, 1981; McIntosh, 1968) is most likely to be internalized in an antihomosexual and sex-role rigid society, utilizing the mechanisms described by Ross et al. (1978). It will be necessary, however, to utilize larger samples that include individuals closer to the heterosexual end of the Kinsey scale before the findings of the present study can be regarded as definitive.

REFERENCES

Banks, A. S. and Gregg, P. M. Grouping political systems: Q-factor analysis of a cross-polity survey. *American Behavioral Scientist*, 1965, *9*, 3-6.

Bem, S. L. The measurement of psychological androgyny. *Journal of Consulting and Clinical Psychology*, 1974, *42*, 155-162.

Fisher, S. and Greenberg, R. P. *The scientific credibility of Freud's theories and therapy.* New York: Basic Books, 1977.

Freud, S. [Some neurotic mechanisms in jealousy, paranoia and homosexuality] (J. Strachey, Ed. and trans.). *The standard edition of the complete psychological works of Sigmund Freud* (Vol. 18). London: Hogarth, 1955. (Originally published, 1922.)

Goode, E. Comments on the homosexual role. *The Journal of Sex Research,* 1981, *17,* 54-65.

Heilbrun, A. B. and Thompson, N. L. Sex role identity and male and female homosexuality. *Sex Roles,* 1977, *3,* 65-79.

Kinsey, A. C., Pomeroy, W. B. and Martin, C. E. *Sexual behavior in the human male.* Philadelphia: W. B. Saunders, 1948.

McIntosh, M. The homosexual role. *Social Problems,* 1968, *16,* 182-192.

McKenzie, N. *Women in Australia.* Melbourne: Cheshire, 1962.

Money, J. Two names, two wardrobes, two personalities. *Journal of Homosexuality,* 1974, *1,* 65-70.

Money, J. and Ehrhardt, A. A. *Man and woman, boy and girl: The differentiation and dimorphism of gender identity from conception to maturity.* Baltimore: Johns Hopkins, 1972.

Money, J. Determinants of human gender identity/role. In J. Money and H. Musaph (Eds.), *Handbook of sexology* (Vol. 1). New York: Elsevier, 1977.

Ross, M. W. Relationship between sex role and sex orientation in homosexual men. *New Zealand Psychologist,* 1975, *4,* 25-29.

Ross, M. W., Rogers, L. J. and McCulloch, H. Stigma, sex and society: A look at gender differentiation and sexual variation. *Journal of Homosexuality,* 1978, *3,* 315-330.

Shively, M. G. and De Cecco, J. P. Components of sexual identity. *Journal of Homosexuality,* 1977, *3,* 41-48.

Sidanius, J., Ekehammar, B. and Ross, M. W. Comparisons of socio-political attitudes between two democratic societies. *International Journal of Psychology,* 1979, *14,* 225-240.

Wilson, G. and Nias, D. *Love's mysteries: The psychology of sexual attraction.* London: Open Books, 1976.

Conceptions of Masculinity and Femininity as a Basis for Stereotypes of Male and Female Homosexuals

Alan Taylor, MA

University of Aberdeen

ABSTRACT. To date the majority of research published in relation to homosexuality has been concerned with the homosexual's problems, and with the etiology of homosexuality. As little as 8% of published research has dealt with attitudes toward homosexuals, and less still has been concerned with perceptions of and beliefs about homosexuals. Existing research on the latter is reviewed, and research is outlined that investigates perceptions of homosexuals. Stereotypes of male and female homosexuals are examined in the context of masculine-feminine traits using the Personality Attributes Questionnaire. Results strongly support the view that sex role definitions are a highly salient reference point for the public definition of homosexuals.

INTRODUCTION

Definitions of stereotypes have included the "picture in the head" that organizes our perceptions of the world (Lippman, 1922), the cognitive structure we act on as if it were a reality (Cauthen, Robinson & Krauss, 1971), and the consensus about the images evoked by a particular label (Katz & Braly, 1933). In addition, while stereotypes can be described as generalizations that help us to order reality, they have nevertheless come to be associated with narow-mindedness on the part of the stereotyper, and inaccuracy on the part of the stereotype (Campbell, 1967). Although individualistic streotypes have been referred to in the literature (Secord & Backman, 1964), the typical research focus has been consensual beliefs, most often assessed in terms of the personality traits associated with a particular group.

Research dealing specifically with stereotypes of homosexuals is quite

Mr. Taylor is in the Department of Psychology, King's College, University of Aberdeen, Old Aberdeen, AB9 2UB, Scotland. Requests for reprints should be sent to him at that address.

The author wishes to express his thanks to John W. Shepherd, Senior Lecturer in Psychology, University of Aberdeen, for his invaluable assistance in the development of this article.

© 1983 by The Haworth Press, Inc. All rights reserved.

37

rare, and the few studies that have been published are not easily organized into a unified commentary. Where one would hope for complementary results and designs as well as a developed theory to predict and explain the related findings, there is instead a wide variety of approaches to the question, and little organizing theory behind it. To date little evidence is available to allow definite comment on the extent and depth of homosexual stereotypes, their nature and function.

Of those studies concerned with stereotypes of homosexuals, the most straightforward is that reported by Simmons (1965). The stereotypes for 5 "deviant" groups were investigated, one of the groups being homosexuals. The 134 respondents (a quota sample with age, education, and sex differences controlled), were asked to mark off traits they thought characterized the 5 groups; a piloted checklist of 70 traits was used. The stereotype was taken to be those items most frequently selected by respondents as characteristic of a particular group. This is the typical approach to stereotype definition, although it is seldom clear where the cut-off point should fall for inclusion in the stereotype. For example, in Simmons' study the percentage agreement on items varied from 10% to 70%—it seems obvious that 70% agreement on an item implies it is part of the public stereotype, but this is less clear when only 10% of the sample agree on an item. The stereotype of homosexuals for this sample included the following (percentage agreement is given in parentheses): sexually abnormal (72%), perverted (52%); mentally ill (40%), maladjusted (40%), effeminate (29%), lonely (22%), insecure (21%), immoral (16%), repulsive (14%), frustrated (14%), weak-minded (12%), lacking self-control (12%), sensual (11%), secretive (11%), oversexed (10%), dangerous (10%), sinful (10%), and sensitive (10%).

Instead of piloting the traits responded to by subjects, Steffensmeier and Steffensmeier (1974) referred in part to previous research for their stereotypic items. They offered their sample of 373 students only three views of homosexuals: that they are psychologically disturbed ("sick"), are easily identified ("swish") and that they are dangerous because they prey on young people ("dangerous"). The descriptions "sick" and "swish" were included because they "seemed prevalent" to the authors, not because they were suggested by their own or others' research. Endorsement of these three beliefs was examined in relation to sex of homosexual target, sex of subject, and a social distance measure in relation to homosexuals. Almost 68% of the sample accepted the "sick" stereotype; 37% endorsed the "dangerous" stereotype, and 20% the "swish" one. The "dangerous" and "swish" stereotypes were attributed more to male than to female homosexuals. In addition tentative support was found for the view that rejection in terms of increased social distance is positively correlated with acceptance of the "dangerous" and "sick" stereotypes.

Staats (1978) asked a sample of 538 undergraduates to identify those traits, in a list of 84, they thought were typical of homosexuals in general. Respondents also rated homosexuals on a social distance scale (after Bogardus, 1925). The more frequently identified attributes for homosexuals were "sensitive" (230 respondents identified this as applicable), "individualistic" (200), "intelligent" (163), "honest" (127), "imaginative" (109), and "neat" (105). Less frequently selected were "reserved" (89), "alert" (89), "kind" (84), "faithful" (78), "courteous" (78), "sophisticated" (73), and "artistic" (70). It was found, using dummy variable analysis, that these adjectives correlated significantly with less social distance from homosexuals. The following were correlated significantly with increased social distance from homosexuals: "cowardly" (87), "sly" (75), "suspicious" (67), "shrewd" (64), "stupid" (60), "impulsive" (60), and "ignorant" (54). These adjectives can be seen as stereotypical because they are the more frequently selected items. The list, however, is restricted to those items that are closely related to social distance measures, which might lead to the exclusion of other aspects of the homosexual stereotype.

Weissbach and Zagon (1975) asked 20 students to rate an interviewee on a videotaped interview: half the subjects were led to believe that he was homosexual, half were not. Respondents rated the target on 10 bipolar scales, and the differences for the two conditions were compared. Five of the scales were selected "to reflect general personality characteristics" that were not thought to differentiate homosexuals and heterosexuals, and the remaining 5 were "believed *a priori*" to be sensitive to homosexual/non-homosexual differences. Significant differences after labelling suggested that the homosexual target was seen as weaker, more feminine, more emotional, more submissive and more unconventional than when he was not labelled homosexual.

In an anticipated interaction paradigm, Gurwitz and Marcus (1978) assessed the effect of homosexual stereotypes on first impressions. In a preliminary study, 40 students rated a list of 77 traits in terms of whether they applied more to homosexual than to heterosexual men and vice versa. An item was defined as stereotypic if more than 75% of the sample agreed that an item was more typical of male homosexuals than male heterosexuals. In this sense male homosexuals were seen as less aggressive and strong than heterosexuals, poorer leaders, more clothes conscious, more gentle, more passive and more theatrical. These and 9 other neutral traits (i.e., rated as applying equally to both target groups), were then used in the anticipated interaction experiment with a sample of 96 students. Five of the so-called neutral traits also led to different ratings for male homosexuals. The homosexual target was rated on these as less calm, less dependable, less honest and less religious than the male heterosexual.

Three studies have referred directly to homosexual stereotypes when studying determinants of homosexual attitudes. Storms (1978) tried to establish whether male homosexuals are disliked because they deviate sexually or because they are perceived to deviate from sex role prescriptions. A sample of 258 students were asked to rate their like/dislike for male targets who were hypo-, hyper- or average masculine, and homosexual or heterosexual. Analysis showed that although sex role deviance was disliked, sexual deviance was disliked more, and Storms suggested that sexual deviance is therefore more important in the evaluation of homosexuals. An interesting result was that masculine homosexual targets were disliked most. Storm explains this by referring to a general expectation that male homosexuals are effeminate, the suggestion being that masculine homosexuals are disliked more than feminine ones because they violate this expectation. In an indirect way this suggests that male homosexuals are perceived as sex role deviants.

Storms' design was adopted in two studies conducted by Laner and Laner (1979, 1980), which included a replication for Lesbian targets. The results were very similar to Storms' in that sex role deviance and sexual deviance were both implicated as bases for disliking homosexuals. One part of their work might be taken as a direct assessment of stereotypes of the targets. Respondents were asked to select, from a pool of 12, three words they thought characterized the various targets in the study. The 12 were selected from a larger pool to reflect varying degrees of "likeableness", i.e., some words were rated as more favorable than others. The words more frequently attributed to male homosexuals for example, were (percentage agreement is given in parentheses) "unappealing" (28%), "inoffensive" (18%), "disagreeable" (15%), "dangerous" (14%), "eccentric" (14%), "hostile" (13%), "agreeable" (12%), and "frivolous" (11%). However, these elicited descriptions of homosexuals are perhaps more useful in clarifying the attitudes toward the various targets in these studies, since they were selected from a pool of likeability adjectives.

The above summarizes the research to date on stereotypes of homosexuals. The stimuli used to elicit responses have varied from 3 items (Steffensmeier and Steffensmeier, 1974) to 84 items (Staats, 1978), from straightforward possession of a trait (Staats, 1978) to degree of possesion of a trait (Gurwitz & Marcus, 1978), from clearly investigating stereotypes of male homosexuals (Weissbach & Zagon, 1975) to failing to distinguish male and female homosexuals by simply referring to "homosexuals" (Simmons, 1965).

Although most of the studies reviewed make certain assumptions about homosexuals on behalf of their respondents, the relevance of these assumptions tends not to be investigated prior to their use in target descriptions. Studies designed to assess respondents' actual beliefs about homosexuals are very rare. When stereotypes have been referred to in the course of other studies, the variety of stereotypes employed has confounded any generalization concerning stereotypes of homosexuals. The variety of approaches to homosexual stereotypes is in sharp contrast to the uniformity of the type of respondents taking part in their studies. With the exception of Simmons' (1965) work, all the studies reviewed have been concerned with students' perceptions of homosexuals; it would be interesting to extend the study of stereotypes of homosexuals beyond those held by the American student population. Most studies have used descriptions of homosexual targets that were not experimentally based—the common reference point has been the experimenter's beliefs about the general population's beliefs about homosexuals. Perhaps the most important problem has been the failure to develop a theory that might better explain and predict the nature of homosexual stereotypes.

IMPLICATIONS FROM RESEARCH ON ATTITUDES TOWARD HOMOSEXUALS FOR RESEARCH ON STEREOTYPES OF HOMOSEXUALS

One of the earliest attitude studies by Smith (1971) tentatively suggested that anti-homosexual individuals may be more cognitively rigid and authoritarian than individuals with more positive attitudes. This might imply a more strict and fixed view of homosexuals on the part of anti-homosexual individuals. Henley and Pincus (1978), referring to their sample of 211 students, reported significant and positive correlations between measures of attitude toward ethnic minorities and attitudes toward homosexuals. Dunbar, Brown and Vuorinen (1973) found that attitudes toward homosexuals correlated moderately with measures of sex-guilt and conservative sexual attitudes, which could be inferred from Smith's study. Again the relationship between attitude and authoritarianism might have implications for stereotypes of homosexuals. Direct comment on these implications was made by Brown and Amoroso (1975), whereby respondents with more negative attitudes tended to stereotype the sexes more; they were also more willing to attribute homosexuality to a male if he exhibited one feminine characteristic. Perhaps this reflects an association among three factors: the positive evaluation of sex-role norms, the assumption that homosexuals violate sex-role norms, and the negative evaluation of those who are believed to deviate from these norms.

This relationship was highlighted in a study by MacDonald and Games (1974) in which a battery of questionnaires was administered to a sample of 197 students. The questionnaires included measures of sexual attitudes, attitudes toward homosexuals and attitudes toward sex-role standards and equality between the sexes. One finding was that greater adherence to traditional sex role prescriptions, and less approval for equality between the sexes, were positively correlated with more negative attitudes toward homosexuals. MacDonald and Games (1974) explained this by suggesting that stigmatizing homosexuality is a means of reducing sex role confusion; that is, by delineating what is acceptable behavior for men and women.

Much of the research following MacDonald and Games has attempted to clarify the extent to which sex role attitudes and sexual attitudes are correlated with attitudes toward homosexuals. For example, Minnegerode (1976), with a sample of 104 students, found that more negative attitudes toward homosexuality were significantly correlated with both conservative sexual attitudes and traditional beliefs about women. Weinberger and Millham (1977) presented results for a sample of 267 students in confirmation of their hypothesis that negative attitudes toward homosexuals are related to beliefs that homosexuals' behavior is incongruent with their anatomical sex. Karr (1978) manipulated the labelling of a confederate as homosexual and observed the differences in reaction toward the target. The 90 male students taking part in the study rated the male labelled "homosexual" as less masculine and less preferred; they also rated the labeller, another confederate, as more sociable and masculine. MacDonald and Moore (1978) administered questionnaires concerning attitudes toward women and homosexuality, as well as a personal sex role inventory, to 88 male homosexuals. Respondents who supported equality between the sexes held more positive attitudes toward homosexuality. Another study on this theme (Weinberger & Millham, 1979) confirmed the relevance of sex role evaluations to the evaluation of homosexuals. Although sex of homosexual target and sex of respondent were found to be relevant to the prediction of attitude score, they concluded that attitudes toward homosexuals were highly correlated with traditional sex role distinctions. And of course Laner and Laner (1979, 1980), following Storms (1978), showed that evaluations of men's and women's sex role behaviors were relevant to the evaluation of homosexuals.

Several articles have attempted to explain the relationship between sex role prescriptions and the evaluation of homosexuals. The most comprehensive analysis has been by Lehne (1976) who begins with several popular beliefs about homosexuals (as revealed by straightforward opinion polls), and an assessment of their validity. The repeated empirical finding is that homosexuals are, in reality, poorly described by popular beliefs, and Lehne suggests that the stereotypes are not simply a function of contact with homosexuals, but are communicated socially, and serve some purpose other than description of the real world. That is, stereotypes reflect the positive evaluation of traditional sex-role behaviors and are the conceptual basis for devaluing deviation from them. Thus, the social function of negative attitudes toward homosexuals is to define the acceptable limits of behavior for men and women. Ample evidence is available to suggest that sex role stereotypes are held by large sections of society (see Broverman, Vogel, Broverman, Clarkson & Rosenkrantz, 1972). Assuming that homosexuals are defined by the public principally in terms of deviations from sex role, one would expect homosexual stereotypes to be as pervasive and stable as stereotypes of men and women in general, since they accentuate the values bound up with prescriptions for masculine and feminine behavior.

The analysis briefly presented here offers one explanation of the repeated finding that measures of sex role evaluation are one of the best predictors of attitudes toward homosexuals. Other commentators (MacDonald, 1974; Morin & Garfinkle, 1978) have also made this point when reviewing the related literature. Although this link has been suggested and tentatively supported, validation of part of the analysis has lagged—to show that sex role evaluations do have some relevance to evaluations of homosexuals one has also to show that homosexuals are believed to be sex role violators. Some of the reported research does suggest that homosexuals are believed to behave like the opposite sex, and several attitude studies have shown that describing homosexual targets in terms of sex role deviance is meaningful for respondents. In addition, attitude research has shown that agreement with traditional sex role prescriptions is an important predictor of negative attitudes toward homosexuals.

The review of the stereotype literature has shown an approach to homosexual stereotypes that has been rather piecemeal, both in terms of technique and supporting theory. The review suggests that the sex role emphasis found in the attitude research is a good starting point for operationalizing and predicting stereotypes of homosexuals. The present study was designed to do just that, i.e., to examine homosexual stereotypes within the domain of masculine and feminine traits.

Measures have been developed to assess beliefs within this domain— from Bem's Sex-Role Inventory (1974) to semantic differential assessments (Reece, 1964), from word association tests (Heilbrun, 1964) to projective tests (May, 1971). Most of the assessments have been concerned with the relative degree to which individuals possess masculine and feminine attributes. The Personality Attributes Questionnaire, developed by Spence, Helmreich and Stapp (1974), has been specifically used to assess stereotypes of masculinity and femininity. The P.A.Q. is a revision of the Sex Role Stereotypes Questionnaire of Rosenkrantz, Vogel, Bee, Broverman and Broverman (1968). Given a large body of validation for the S.R.S.Q., and the recency of the P.A.Q., as well as its specific use in the assessment of stereotypes, it seemed preferable to use the P.A.Q. scale. Another reason for its adoption is that it is in the form of 55 bipolar 5 point scales, which allows the comparison of homosexual and non-homosexual targets along a continuum, as distinct from other measures that are concerned with presence or absence of an attribute.

In general terms the study was concerned with stereotypes of male and female homosexuals, their differences and their relationship to stereotypes of non-homosexual men and women. More specifically it was expected that female and male homosexuals would be rated significantly differently than their heterosexual counterparts. It was not clear whether mean ratings for the homosexual targets would fall between those for heterosexual men and women, or whether homosexuals would be rated more extremely; i.e., the precise nature of the sex role deviance was not clear. However, as the review above suggests, it seemed likely that a major trend would be for male homosexuals to be rated less masculine/more feminine than heterosexual men, and for female homosexuals to be rated less feminine/more masculine than heterosexual women.

METHOD

Respondents

A group of 103 adults was randomly selected from a pool of subjects affiliated with the Psychology Department. This pool of several hundred adults included no students, but was made up of male and female adults recruited from the general population of the City of Aberdeen. Ages within the sample ranged from 17 to 64 years, the mean age being 42. Reflecting the distribution of the subject pool, there were 64 women and 39 men in the sample. Almost all of the subjects came from the city of Aberdeen, and most had remained at school until 16 years of age. The majority of the sample had skilled or white collar backgrounds.

Procedure

Respondents were provided with four copies of the Personality Attributes Questionnaire; each copy bore one of four group labels: "men," "women," "male homosexuals," or "lesbians." Respondents were asked to rate each group on the P.A.Q. according to what they thought applied to most members of each group.

Three factors had to be considered in this procedure. First, at least some subjects might have been reluctant to cooperate if they believed their ratings were being taken to mean that they, the subjects, thought that every member of the group was exactly as their rating suggested. Therefore, it was made clear that this was not the way the scales would be interpreted, and that it would be assumed their ratings applied to a majority of the target group members. Second, possible order effects for the four sets of scales had to be countered by randomizing across the sample the order in which the groups were rated. Third, confusion might have arisen from the fact that homosexual men are a logical subset of all men. It was pointed out, therefore, that "men" referred to those men who were not homosexual and "women" referred to those women who were not heterosexual. That is, comparisons were being made between heterosexuals and homosexuals, as well as between males and females within these groups.

RESULTS

The sample's ratings for each item were subjected to analysis of variance, with the intention that differences between means would be investigated if significant F values were obtained. In fact, the F values for all the items were significant beyond the 0.001 level. The means for the homosexual targets were compared, and their relationship to the means for "men" and "women" was also examined.

Mean Rating Differences for the Targets "Male Homosexuals" and "Lesbians"

Table 1 shows the probability values associated with the differences in rating means for the 2 homosexual targets. In all, "male homosexuals" were rated significantly differently than "lesbians" on 41 of the P.A.Q. items.

Two sets of stereotypes can be derived from the items where the two homosexual targets were rated significantly differently than one another: the more straightforward involves describing each target group in terms of the item pole its mean was nearest to. The stereotype of "male homosexuals" would therefore be that they are "needful of others' approval, not runners of the show, helpful to others, expressive of tender feelings" and so on. Similarly, "lesbians" would be described stereotypically as "not needful of others' approval, runners of the show,

TABLE 1:   SELECTED MEAN COMPARISONS BETWEEN PAIRS OF TARGETS

Item from P.A.Q. Fem. pole (1) Masc. pole (5)	Mean MH	Mean L	Sig. of Mean Differences			Cross Gender Hypothesis
			MH-L	MH-M	L-W	
Needful of others's approval/ indifferent to	2.8	3.1	ns	ns	**	✓
never sees self running the show/always does	2.8	3.3	**	**	**	✓
very helpful to others/not helpful	2.4	2.8	**	ns	**	✓
not ambitious/very ambitious	3.0	3.3	**	**	ns	✓
ignorant of ways of world/ knows ways of	3.6	3.6	ns	ns	**	x
cries very easily/never cries	2.9	3.1	ns	**	**	✓
expresses tender feelings/ never does	2.0	2.6	**	**	**	✓
very submissive/very dominant	2.8	3.5	**	**	**	✓
goes to pieces under pressure/ does not	2.8	3.2	**	**	ns	✓
very kind/not at all kind	2.2	2.7	**	ns	**	✓
not self confident/very self confident	2.7	3.3	**	**	**	✓
likes children/dislikes children	2.8	3.1	*	**	**	✓
very quiet/very loud	2.5	3.2	**	**	**	✓
not aggressive/very aggressive	2.5	3.3	**	**	**	✓
never hide emotions/always hide emotions	2.7	3.2	**	**	**	✓
feelings easily hurt/not easily hurt	2.2	2.7	**	**	**	✓
not interested in sex/very interested	3.6	3.4	ns	**	ns	x
very creative/not very creative	2.2	2.8	**	**	**	✓
very timid/not at all timid	2.9	3.5	**	**	**	✓
not able with mechanical things/ able with	2.8	2.9	ns	**	**	✓
excitable in major crisis/ not excitable in	2.6	3.1	**	**	*	✓
not independent/very independent	3.2	3.8	**	**	**	✓

TABLE 1 (continued)

Item from P.A.Q Fem. pole (1) Masc. pole (5)	Mean MH	Mean L	Sig. of Mean Differences			Cross Gender Hypothesis
			MH-L	MH-M	L-W	
understanding of others/not understanding	2.3	2.8	**	**	**	✓
not competitive/very competitive	3.0	3.3	**	**	*	✓
able to devote self to others/ not able to	2.5	2.8	*	**	**	✓
not at all outgoing/very outgoing	3.1	3.2	ns	**	ns	✓
never takes a stand/always takes a stand	3.1	3.5	**	**	**	✓
excitable in a minor crisis/ not excitable	2.7	3.3	**	**	ns	✓
not good at sports/very good at sports	2.6	3.3	**	**	**	✓
home-oriented/very worldly	3.1	3.2	ns	ns	**	✓
not intellectual/very intellectual	3.5	3.3	*	**	ns	x
very considerate/not at all considerate	2.3	2.9	**	**	**	✓
feels inferior/feels superior	2.7	3.0	*	**	ns	✓
very tactful/completely tactless	2.6	3.0	**	**	**	✓
not forward/very forward	2.9	3.3	**	**	**	✓
strong need for security/little need for	1.9	2.1	ns	**	**	✓
very passive/very active	3.0	3.4	**	**	ns	✓
warm in relations with others/ cold in	2.3	2.9	**	**	**	✓
dislikes maths and science/ likes them	3.1	3.1	ns	**	**	x
not adventurous/very adventurous	3.0	3.3	**	**	**	✓
very religious/not religious	3.2	3.3	ns	ns	**	✓
has difficulty in making decisions/does not	2.9	3.1	ns	**	*	✓
not skilled in business/very skilled	3.2	3.2	ns	**	**	x
very emotional/not emotional	2.0	2.5	**	**	**	✓

TABLE 1 (continued)

Item from P.A.Q. Fem. pole (1) Masc. pole (5)	Mean MH	Mean L	Sig. of Mean Differences			Cross Gender Hypothesis
			MH-L	MH-M	L-W	
strong conscience/no conscience	2.8	2.8	ns	ns	**	x
very neat/not at all neat	2.0	2.8	**	**	**	√
not at all outspoken/very outspoken	2.8	3.3	**	**	**	√
very gentle/very rough	2.2	2.9	**	**	**	√
never acts as leader/always does	2.6	3.2	**	**	**	√
aware of others' feelings/not aware of	2.1	2.5	**	**	**	√
very grateful/not at all grateful	2.6	3.0	**	*	**	√
enjoys art and music/does not	2.0	2.6	**	**	**	√
easily influenced/not easily influenced	3.1	3.6	**	**	**	√
gives up easily/never gives up easily	3.2	3.6	**	**	ns	√

*Table notes:

"ns" = the difference between means was not significant

"*" = the difference between means was significant beyond the 0.05 level

"**" = the difference between means was significant beyond the 0.01 level

"√" = the mean for male homosexuals was nearer the feminine pole, and the mean for lesbians was nearer the masculine pole

"x" = the pattern for "√" was not sustained

NB: That the order of the poles in Table 1 is Feminine first, and Masculine second, ie. the most feminine rating is "1", and the most masculine rating is "5". When presented to subjects 25 of the items had these poles reversed, ie. the most masculine rating was a "1", most feminine a "5". The means for these 25 items were reflected to allow a simpler presentation of the results.

unhelpful, not expressive of tender feelings" and so on. The second set of stereotypes involves a comparative description of the two homosexual targets for each item. In this way the stereotype of "male homosexuals" would be, for example, that they are "more needful of others' approval than 'lesbians'"; "lesbians" could similarly be the focus of comparisons. The full stereotype for the homosexual targets can be seen by referring to all the items in Table 1 where "male homosexuals" were rated significantly differently than "lesbians."

The Relationship between Homosexual Target Means and Heterosexual Target Means

The description of stereotypes of homosexuals detailed in the above section leaves out an important pattern in the ratings for the four groups, one which substantiates the general hypothesis suggested earlier; *viz.*, that homosexuals are defined as sex-role deviants. Simple confirmation of this hypothesis would involve, for example, "male homosexuals" being rated significantly differently than "men," and "lesbians" being rated significantly differently than "women." Since the targets "men" and "women" were taken to represent heterosexual men and women in general, and the items in the P.A.Q. were devised to reflect general impressions of masculinity/femininity, it follows that such differences reflect a perception of homosexuals as sex-role deviants.

Table 1 shows that "male homosexuals" were in fact rated significantly differently than "men" and "lesbians" than "women," on the majority of items. The differences were significant for "male homosexuals"/"men" comparisons on 47 out of the 54 items and for "lesbians"/"women" on 45 of the items. This is strong evidence for the hypothesis that the homosexual targets were seen as sex-role deviants.

Another way of describing the rating pattern for the homosexual targets relates the homosexual target means to the pre-defined masculine and feminine pole of each item. With this reference point one would be interested to see if "male homosexuals" were nearer the feminine pole of each item, and "lesbians" nearer the masculine pole. The results of this simple analysis are shown in the last column of Table 1. On 48 occasions the "cross-gender hypothesis" was supported for the perception of homosexuals; i.e., "male homosexuals" were rated more feminine than "lesbians," and "lesbians" more masculine than "male homosexuals." Another assessment of this cross-gender pattern can be done by checking whether the mean for "male homosexuals" is lower than the mean for "lesbians" (given that the most feminine rating is one, the most masculine, 5).

The cross-gender hypothesis was not supported on six items; on four occasions the means for "male homosexuals" and "lesbians" were the same, and on two (interest in sex, being intellectual or not) "male homosexuals" were rated more masculine than "lesbians." (Note that for these and all the other items the means for "men" were nearer the masculine pole, and those for "women" nearer the feminine pole.)

DISCUSSION

A review of the literature on stereotypes of homosexuals reveals an inconsistency of approach and an accompanying lack of organizing theory. Examination of public stereotypes of male homosexuals has been rare and rarer still has been the assessment of stereotypes of lesbians. The present study was concerned with a fuller assessment of both male and female homosexual stereotypes as well as with locating such an examination within a context that might serve to explain the content of the stereotypes.

The homosexual targets in the present study were rated differently on a large number of items, confirming that homosexual stereotypes existed for this sample, and that male and female homosexuals were perceived differently. An important point is that the majority of the differences are better described as comparisons. That is, there are few items where the homosexual targets are rated differently than all other targets; typically they are distinct from one another and rated similarly to their non-homosexual and opposite sex target. Thus the more accurate representation of the stereotypes is in the form of "more emotional than men," or "more emotional than lesbians," for example. Since all measures of stereotypes have their origins in item pools that are thought to characterize people in general, it seems a more reasonable assessment of stereotypes to ask to what degree the target group possesses an attribute, rather than whether or not it possesses the attribute at all. Placing homosexual stereotypes in this context has only been addressed in the most recent studies, and even then the contexts have been quite restricted. The present study has attempted to provide a full and relevant context for homosexual stereotypes.

One problem with providing a set of scales for eliciting stereotypes is that the elicited responses may be more a function of the scales used than of individuals' perceptions of the target group. However, subjects in the present study were clearly informed that they should rate according to what they believed, and that it was not a formal test of knowledge. If the responses were simply a function of the scales, it is unclear why responses were so consistent across this diverse sample of adults. Another important point is the meaningfulness of the results in relation to other studies concerned with attitudes toward homosexuals, which could be seen as predicting the pattern obtained so consistently here.

For several years evidence has been available to suggest that sex role evaluations are a major predictor of attitudes toward homosexuals. It has seemed obvious, to the extent of being left unresearched, that the correlation between the two involves the belief that homosexuals are sex role deviants. That is, those who value traditional sex roles devalue homosexuals because they perceive them to be role deviants, and those who do not value the roles so highly do not care. But the necessary antecedent for explaining the relevance of sex role attitudes, i.e., perceiving homosexuals as sex role deviants, has not itself been substantiated.

This is significant for several reasons. The present study shows not only that stereotypes of male and female homosexuals exist but also that they are predictable, for reasons outlined above. Most of the studies to date have simply assumed the perception of homosexuals as sex-role deviants in the course of explaining the relevance of sex-role evaluations to attitudes toward homosexuals. This assumption, which might otherwise be characterized as the stereotype researchers have of the public's stereotype, has had important consequences for research. In the work of Laner and Laner (1979; 1980), Storms, (1978) and Steffensmeier and Steffensmeier (1974), for example, the cross-gender perception has been used without investigating its prevalence and relevance.

It is clear that sex role evaluations (among other variables) are related to attitudes toward homosexuals. Research, however, has tended to neglect the respondents' actual perceptions of homosexuals by giving them descriptions selected *a priori* or by neglecting their perceptions altogether. We have had evidence to suggest that attitudes toward homosexuals are highly correlated with sex role attitudes. Perhaps more importantly for other research, the present study has substantiated the presumption that the necessary mediating belief, i.e., that homosexuals behave like the opposite sex, is alive and well.

Finally, a growing body of research (Bell & Weinberg, 1978; Masters & Johnson, 1979; Weinberg & Williams, 1975) clearly contradicts these public stereotypes of homosexuals. It is not the case, as most of the present respondents believe, that most homosexuals behave like the opposite sex. A striking feature of the present data is the consistency of this belief within a varied sample of adults responding to a large number of items. It is possibly the case that this reflects a socially transmitted veiw of homosexuals, as Lehne (1976) and others have suggested, and a well-popularized myth concerning the true nature of homosexuals. The finer points of a theory of homosexual stereotypes will have to deal with the development of these stereotypes in relation to media portrayals, for example, and personal contact with homosexuals. In addition it might explain the persistence of this inaccurate representation of homosexuals. It would also be of interest to examine the relationships among sets of attitudes (toward homosexuals, sex roles, etc.), contact with homosexuals, and deviations from the modal stereotypes documented here.

REFERENCES

Bell, A. P. & Weinberg, M. S. *Homosexualities: A study of diversity among men and women.* London: Mitchell Beazley, 1978.
Bem, S. L. The measurement of psychological androgyny. *Journal of Consulting and Clinical Psychology,* 1974, *42,* 155-162

Bogardus, E. S. Measuring social distance. *Journal of Applied Sociology,* 1925, *9,* 299-308.

Broverman, I. K., Vogel, S. R., Broverman, D. M., Clarkson, F. E. & Rosenkrantz, P. S. Sex roles stereotypes: A current appraisal. *Journal of Social Issues,* 1972, *28,* 59-78.

Brown, M. & Amoroso, D. M. Attitudes toward homosexuality among West Indian male and female college students. *Journal of Social Psychology,* 1975, *97,* 163-168.

Campbell, D. T. Stereotypes and the perception of group differences. *American Psychologist,* 1967, *22,* 817-829.

Cauthen, N. R., Robinson, I. E. & Krauss, H. H. Stereotypes: A review of the literature 1926-1968. *Journal of Social Psychology,* 1971, *81,* 103-125.

Dunbar, J., Brown, M. & Vuorinen, S. Attitudes toward homosexuality among Brazilian and Canadian college students. *Journal of Social Psychology,*1973, *90,* 173-183.

Gurwitz, S. B. & Marcus, M. Effects of anticipated interaction, sex and homosexual stereotypes on first impressions. *Journal of Applied Social Psychology,* 1978, *8,* 47-56.

Heilbrun, A. B. Conformity to masculinity-femininity stereotypes and ego identity in adolescents. *Psychological Reports,* 1964, *14,* 351-357.

Henley, N. M. & Pincus, F. Interrelationship of sexist, racist and anti-homosexual attitudes. *Psychological Reports,* 1978, *42,* 83-90.

Karr, R. G. Homosexual labelling and the male role. *Journal of Social Issues,* 1978, *34*(3), 73-83.

Katz, D. & Braly, K.W. Racial stereotypes of 100 college students. *Journal of Abnormal and Social Psychology,* 1933, *28,* 280-290.

Laner, M. R. & Laner, R. H. Personal style or sexual preference? Why gay men are disliked. *International Review of Modern Sociology,* 1979, *9,* 215-228.

Laner, M. R. & Laner, R. H. Sexual preference or personal style? Why lesbians are disliked. *Journal of Homosexuality,* 1980, *5,* 339-356.

Lehne, G. K, Homophobia among men. In D. David & R. Brannon (Eds.), *The 49% majority: The male sex role.* Reading, MA: Addison-Wesley, 1976.

Lippman, W. *Public Opinion.* New York: Harcourt Brace, 1922.

MacDonald, A. P. The importance of sex role to gay liberation. *Homosexual Counseling Journal,* 1974, *1,* 169-180.

MacDonald, A. P. & Games, R. Some characteristics of those who hold positive and negative attitudes toward homosexuals. *Journal of Homosexuality,* 1974, *1,* 9-27.

MacDonald, G. J. & Moore, R. J. Sex role self concepts of homosexual men and their attitudes toward both women and male homosexuality. *Journal of Homosexuality,* 1978, *4,* 3-14.

Masters, R. & Johnson, V. *Homosexuality in perspective.* Boston: Little, Brown, 1979.

May, R. R. A method for studying the development of gender identity. *Developmental Psychology,* 1971, *5,* 484-487.

Minnegerode, F. A. Attitudes toward homosexuality: Feminist attitudes and sexual conservatism. *Sex Roles,* 1976, *2,* 347-352.

Morin, S. F. Heterosexual bias in psychological research on lesbianism and male homosexuality. *American Psychologist,* 1977, *37,* 629-637.

Morin, S. F. & Garfinkle, E. M. Male homophobia. *Journal of Social Issues,* 1978, *34*(1), 29-47.

Reece, M. M. Masculinity-femininity: A factor analytic study. *Psychological Reports,* 1964, *14,* 123-139.

Rosenkrantz, P. S., Vogel, S. R., Bee, H., Broverman, I. K. & Broverman, D. M. Sex role stereotypes and self concepts in college students. *Journal of Consulting and Clinical Psychology,* 1968, *32,* 287-295.

Secord, D. F. & Backman, C. W. *Social Psychology.* New York: McGraw-Hill, 1964.

Simmons, J. L. Public stereotypes of deviants. *Social Problems,* 1965, *13,* 223-232.

Smith, K. T. Homophobia: A tentative personality profile. *Psychological Reports,* 1971, *29,* 1091-1094.

Spence, J. T., Helmreich, R. & Stapp, J. The Personal Attributes Questionnaire: A measure of sex role stereotypes and masculinity and femininity. *Catalogue of Selected Documents in Psychology,* 1974, *4,* 43-44.

Staats, G. R. Stereotype content and social distance: Changing views of homosexuality. *Journal of Homosexuality,* 1978, *4,* 15-28.

Steffensmeier, C. & Steffensmeier, R. Sex differences in reactions to homosexuals: Research continuities and further developments. *Journal of Sex Research,* 1974, *10,* 52-67.

Storms, M. D. Attitudes toward homosexuality and femininity in men. *Journal of Homosexuality,* 1978, *3,* 257-263.

Weinberg, M. S. & Williams, C. S. *Male homosexuals: Their problems and adaptions.* (Revised edition). New York: Penguin, 1975.

Weinberger, L. E. & Millham, J. Sexual preference, sex role appropriateness and restriction of social access. *Journal of Homosexuality,* 1977, *2,* 343-347.

Weinberger, L. E. & Millham, J. Attitudinal homophobia and support of traditional sex roles. *Journal of Homosexuality,* 1979, *4,* 237-246.

Weissbach, T. A. & Zagon, G. The effect of deviant group membership upon impressions of personality. *Journal of Social Psychology,* 1975, *95,* 263-266.

Sex Role Stereotypes, Gender Identity and Parental Relationships in Male Homosexuals and Heterosexuals

C. Anne Mallen, BA (Hons.)

University of Melbourne

ABSTRACT. The sex-role stereotypes held by heterosexual and homosexual men were examined by comparing their Repertory Grid scores. It was found that homosexual men held less rigid sex-role stereotypes than heterosexuals. Degree of opposite-sex identification was marginally greater in homosexuals, but neither group showed strong masculine or feminine stereotypic identification. Homosexual men perceived themselves as psychologically more distant from their fathers than did their heterosexual counterparts; this was probably an effect of homosexuality rather than a cause.

Elucidation of the sex-role stereotypes held by homosexuals is a subject which has been largely ignored by social science researchers. Various explanations have been proposed regarding this scarcity of information (Thompson & McCandless, 1976). Since sex-role stereotyping is a relatively new area of investigation, researchers are often too occupied with elucidating sex-role stereotypes held by heterosexuals to concern themselves with a minority group that apparently does not fit the basic pattern.

It would appear advisable to rectify this neglect in the light of recent findings. For example, several researchers have noted that homosexuals of both sexes have tended to rate themselves differently from heterosexuals of their sex on the dimensions of psychological masculinity and femininity (for a review of this literature, see West, 1977). Thompson, Schwartz, McCandless and Edwards (1973) found that homosexual males tended to obtain more "feminine" scores on a variety of tests, and to describe less masculine interests and attitudes than did heterosexual male control subjects.

This research formed part of a BA (Hons.) thesis in psychology at the University of Melbourne. The author would like to thank Drs. Roger Holden and Michael Ross for their help and encouragement with this study.

Reprint requests should be addressed to Anne Mallen, 17 Barrington Avenue, Kew, 3101, Australia.

© 1983 by The Haworth Press, Inc. All rights reserved.

55

These tentative findings may indicate that male homosexuals do not perceive themselves in the sex-role stereotypic way that male heterosexuals have been found to do. If this proposition is accepted, it follows that male homosexuals might be expected to extend their self-perceptions to perceptions of others. Sex-role stereotypes exist at least partially to enable individuals to relate to strangers and acquaintances in a way that is mutually understood. If homosexuals deviate from the conventional way of relating, they would be expected to encounter some hostility from the predominantly heterosexual society, since they are projecting discrepant expectations. Contemporary homophile groups present a challenge to prevailing social values in their increased demands for equality of social and legal status with heterosexuals. This challenge could be met either by society changing its basic stereotypic expectations in order to accommodate homosexuals, or by homosexuals changing to conform more closely to societal expectations. The latter situation appears unlikely, since many homophile groups assert that the basis of discrimination against homosexuals is society's rigid adherence to traditional masculine and feminine roles. Investigation of the sex-role stereotypes held by homosexuals has some importance, therefore, and it constitutes a major focus of the present study. Closely related to the concept of sex-role stereotyping is the notion of gender identity, since gender identity is at least partially based upon perceptions of masculine and feminine roles within one's culture.

The majority of available evidence (Bem, 1974; Lunneborg, 1970; Elman, Press & Rosenkrantz, Note 1) suggests that male heterosexuals have described themselves in stereotypically masculine terms. From this it may be assumed that the gender identity of heterosexuals (as measured in terms of masculinity and femininity) to a large degree reflects cultural stereotypes.

Investigators of the gender identity of male and female homosexuals have attempted to show that, on a variety of psychometeric measures, both groups produce responses that are atypical of their own sex and more typical of the opposite sex. Results have been variable.

Thompson et al. (1973) compared male homosexuals with their heterosexual counterparts on various self-rated masculinity-femininity measures. Homosexuals typically obtained more feminine scores on the measures, as well as described less masculine interests and attitudes from childhood onwards. Saghir and Robins (1973) found that male homosexuals differed from male heterosexuals in the high frequency (67%) with which homosexuals reported girlish tendencies in childhood and adolescence, and the low frequency (3%) with which heterosexuals recalled such tendencies. The Bem Sex Role Inventory (BSRI) (Bem, 1974) has been used to compare the gender identities of homosexual and heterosexual males. Bernard and Epstein (1978) and Hooberman

(1976) reported that male heterosexuals obtained higher masculinity scores on the BSRI, while male homosexuals obtained higher femininity scores. More male homosexuals were sex-typed as feminine and androgynous; more heterosexuals as masculine.

Gender identity has traditionally been associated with relationships with parents, although more recently Biller (1971) and others have emphasized the role of the father over that of the mother. Fathers have generally been found to insist more than mothers on sex-appropriate behavior from children of both sexes, particularly boys. Thompson and McCandless (1976), reviewing the literature, report that homosexual sons have tended to describe their fathers in more negative terms than have heterosexual sons. Similarly, Evans (1969), Stephan (1973) and Thompson et al. (1973), using different methodologies, have suggested that relationships between homosexual males and their fathers tend to be more distant and cold than those of heterosexuals. In a study of identification of homosexual men with their fathers, Chang and Block (1960) confirmed this, and Stephan (1973) found that homosexuals tended to have less satisfactory male models as children.

On the other hand, several studies (Greenblatt, 1967; Schofield, 1965) have found no such differences in homosexuals as compared with heterosexuals. The picture emerging from studies of relations between male homosexuals and their mothers is inconsistent and difficult to interpret. The pattern of a close, emotionally intense relationship reported by Thompson et al. (1973), Saghir and Robins (1973) and Stephan (1973) has been contradicted by other studies (Bene, 1965; Siegelman, 1974). It is unclear whether relationships of homosexual males with their mothers follow any particular pattern.

It is obvious that these highly complex and difficult areas require more thorough investigation. It may be that male homosexuals do tend to perceive themselves in terms more typical of the opposite sex, but the picture is far from clear. The measure used in the present study, a modified Kelly (1955) repertory grid allows the researcher to gain some insight into the sex role stereotypes gender identity of homosexual and heterosexual subjects. By examining scores of all subjects on this measure, it should be possible to clarify the areas to some degree.

METHOD

Subjects

The sample consisted of 60 subjects. Each subject was assigned to a sex preference group (N = 30) on the basis of self-ratings on the seven-point Kinsey scale (Kinsey, Pomeroy & Martin, 1948). This scale ranges from 0 (exclusively heterosexual) to 6 (exclusively homosexual). Subjects who rated themselves as 0, 1 or 2 were considered heterosexual; those who rated themselves as 4, 5, or 6 were considered homosexual. No subject rated himself as 3.

An attempt was made to obtain a more representative cross-section of the homosexual population than has been sampled in the majority of previous studies. Sources included university homophile groups, a homosexual activist group, and a homosexual church group, plus a number of personal contacts. The majority of heterosexual subjects were undergraduates from the University of Melbourne. The remainder included a group of graduate teachers, and a number of personal contacts.

Subjects from the two groups were matched as far as possible for age and education level. Some limitations were imposed by the difficulty of obtaining homosexual subjects. The mean age of heterosexual males was 23.1 ± 5.7 years; mean age of homosexual males was 24.2 ± 3.8 years. Of the heterosexual sample, 26 males had received some tertiary education, while 27 male homosexuals had done so. All remaining subjects had completed at least five years of secondary education.

Research Instrument

General demographic data were obtained relating to subjects' age, sexual preference and educational level. The rating grid, which consisted of a 14 x 14 matrix, was derived from Kelly (1955, p. 270) and recommended by Fransella and Bannister (1977, p. 40). Along the top of the grid were listed 14 role titles (elements); down the left hand side were listed 14 pairs of bipolar adjectives (constructs). Both elements and constructs were assumed to be related to aspects of masculinity, femininity and sex-role stereotyping. Elements were selected on the basis of results of a previous pilot study, while constructs were derived from a cross-section of relevant literature.

Selection of Elements

A pilot study was conducted in order to ensure that role titles used in the final rating grid were relevant to subjects' conceptions of masculinity, femininity and sex-role stereotyping. Sixty first-year psychology students from the University of Melbourne were asked to indicate which of a list of 33 role titles seemed relevant to their personal notions of masculinity and femininity. Space was provided in which they could add any additional titles. Subjects were also asked to indicate whether or not each role title referred to a person they knew. This was an attempt to increase the probability that subjects would be able to match role titles in the final grid with individuals with whom they were personally familiar (as recommended by Kelly, 1955). Instructions to subjects were standardized.

There were two criteria for selection of grid elements. First, each role title had to describe a person familiar to a least 80 percent of pilot study subjects. From this reduced list, the 12 role titles which were endorsed by the greatest number of subjects as relevant to their notions of masculinity and/or femininity were selected for inclusion. Ordering of male/female and female/male in pairs of role titles (such as ADMIRED MALE/ADMIRED FEMALE: CLOSE FEMALE FRIEND/ CLOSE MALE FRIEND) was interchanged in the final grid to avoid response set biases. Final elements were Mother, Father, very masculine male, very feminine female, athletic person, close male friend, close female friend, ex-boy/girlfriend, admired female, admired male, brother, spouse or current boy/girlfriend. Two additional elements were selected for the final rating grid: SELF and IDEAL SELF. These were included as a means of investigating both gender identity and perceptions of parents. Their selection follows Ryle and Lunghi (1972).

Selection of Constructs

Constructs were selected on the basis of assumed relevance to the present study. All adjectives were derived from the literature on sex-role stereotyping and masculinity/femininity of heterosexuals and homosexuals. The constructs included were as follows: Dependent - Independent, Unconventional - Conventional, Cruel - Kind, Extraverted - Introverted, Non-aggressive - Aggressive, Rough - Gentle, Unrestricted - Restricted, Passive - Active, Not influential - Influential, Controlled - Spontaneous, Unattractive - Attractive, Has trouble expressing emotions - Expresses emotions easily, Not compassionate - Compassionate, Not ambitious - Ambitious.

Procedure

The questionnaire was administered by the experimenter to small groups of subjects (N = 10). This allowed for a relaxed atmosphere, and enabled the experimenter to answer any queries during the 45 minutes (approximately) required to complete the questionnaire. Five individuals refused to participate in the study: The most frequently stated reason was lack of time to fill in the questionnaire. A standardized set of instructions was read to all subjects.

RESULTS AND DISCUSSION

Because of the complexity of data from the present study, the presentation has been simplified by dividing it into sections.

Presentation will adhere to the following pattern. Repertory grid data in terms of principal components will be presented first, after which attention will focus upon evaluation of masculinity and femininity. Then the grid element SELF and its inter-relationships with other elements and constructs will be examined. This discussion will be extended to a consideration of the relation of SELF and IDEAL SELF.

With regard to principal components analyses, it would be expected that if sex-role stereotyping occurred, then female role figures would be attributed stereotypic feminine characteristics and male figures, stereotypic masculine characteristics. Thus, if figures were intercorrelated across constructs and factor analyzed, one should find a large principal component (first or second) associated with such stereotypic contrasts. Since our interest lies in comparing two whole groups, it would be appropriate to carry out correlations on the pooled values within each group available through Slater's (1972) program *SERIES*. If, as predicted, stereotyping is particularly characteristic of heterosexuals, then it would provide a greater source of variance in their grid data. This would be evident as a larger and more pervasive sex-role stereotypic component.

It is usual to find two principal components of significance in such pooled data. Evidence of this lies in Table 1, which presents the order of magnitude on the first three principal components of present subject groups. Once one component can be identified with sex-role stereotypic contrasts, interest attaches to the other, which provides indications of more general aspects of the outlook of each group.

Principal Components Analyses

Figures 1 and 2 present the loadings of elements and constructs on the first two principal components of homosexual and heterosexual males respectively. The discussion is based upon loadings greater than .3 or less than − .3.

Since elements and constructs were selected on the basis of their sex-role stereotypic nature, it was expected that a major component

Table 1
Per Cent of Variance Accounted for by the First Three Principal
Components of Each Group of Subjects

Component Number	Per Cent of Variance	
	Heterosexual Males	Homosexual Males
1	41	45
2	34	34
3	10	9

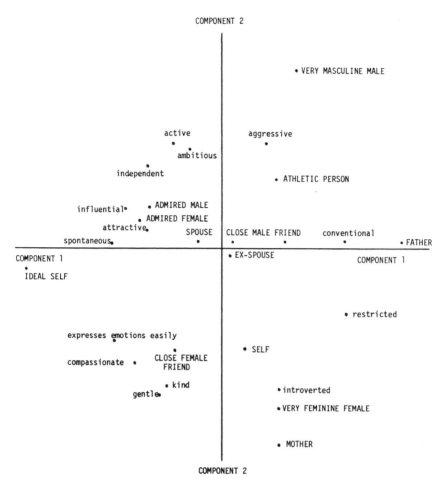

Figure 1: Loadings of Elements and Constructs on the First Two Principal Components of Homosexual Males.

would express sex-role stereotypic contrasts. In the case of heterosexual males, this was true of their first component. Elements and constructs loaded according to a sex-role stereotypic pattern. Male figures (for example, VERY MASCULINE MALE, ADMIRED MALE, IDEAL SELF, ATHLETIC PERSON) had high positive loadings, while female figures (for example, VERY FEMININE FEMALE, EX-SPOUSE, MOTHER, CLOSE FEMALE FRIEND) had high negative loadings. Constructs with high positive loadings, which included ROUGH, AGGRESSIVE, AMBITIOUS, ACTIVE, INFLUENTIAL and INDEPENDENT, were descriptive of the masculine stereotype. Those with high negative loadings, such as GENTLE, PASSIVE, DEPENDENT, INTROVERTED, KIND and NOT AMBITIOUS, were descriptions of the feminine stereotype.

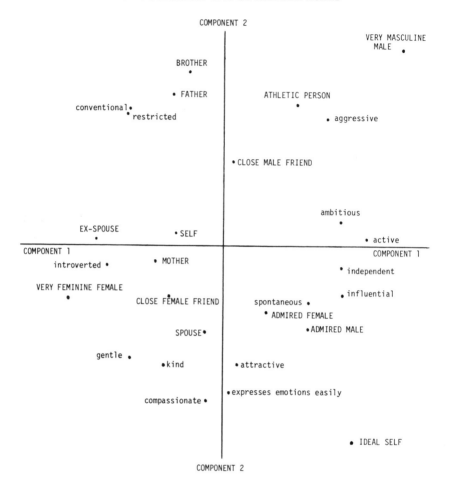

Figure 2: Loadings of Elements and Constructs on the First Two Principal
           Components of Heterosexual Males

The second component of the heterosexual male group could be described as an introceptive dimension, with the introceptive pole being considered desirable (as shown by the high loadings of IDEAL SELF, ADMIRED MALE and ADMIRED FEMALE). Constructs with high loadings included ATTRACTIVE, COMPASSIONATE, EXPRESSES EMOTIONS EASILY, KIND and GENTLE. The non-introceptive pole was characterized as AGGRESSIVE, CRUEL, NOT COMPASSIONATE, NOT ATTRACTIVE and CONVENTIONAL and was associated with such figures as VERY MASCULINE MALE, ATHLETIC PERSON, FATHER and BROTHER.

The expected sex-role stereotypic dimension of homosexual males was a smaller second component. Male figures (for example, VERY MASCULINE MALE, ADMIRED MALE) had high positive loadings, while female figures (for example, VERY FEMININE FEMALE, MOTHER, CLOSE FEMALE FRIEND) had high negative loadings. MOTHER was perceived as closer to the feminine pole than was VERY FEMININE FEMALE. Constructs followed a sex-role stereotypic pattern, with AGGRESSIVE, ACTIVE, AMBITIOUS and ROUGH having high positive loadings; PASSIVE, NON-AGGRESSIVE and GENTLE high negative loadings.

The first component of homosexual males could be labelled an expressive dimension, with the expressive pole (highly correlated with IDEAL SELF, ADMIRED MALE and ADMIRED FEMALE) being admired. Rejection of the element FATHER has shown by its extremely high negative loading. Constructs with high positive loadings included SPONTANEOUS, EXPRESSES EMOTIONS EASILY, EXTRA-VERTED and UNRESTRICTED, while the non-expressive pole was characterized as RESTRICTED, INTROVERTED, CONTROLLED and HAS TROUBLE EXPRESSING EMOTIONS.

From the principal components analyses, it can be seen that both homosexual and heterosexual males responded to a series of sex-role stereotypic figures and attributes by producing the expected stereotypic dimension. However, stereotypic perceptions appeared to be more important to heterosexual than homosexual males. Evidence of this lay in the order of magnitude of the groups' respective sex-role stereotypic components. In the case of heterosexual males, their first component expressed stereotypic contrasts. For homosexuals, this was true of their smaller second component, and furthermore, almost half of the elements (CLOSE MALE FRIEND, FATHER, BROTHER, SPOUSE, IDEAL SELF) failed to load on the dimension. It seemed that the less familiar figures on the grid (for example, VERY MASCULINE MALE, VERY FEMININE FEMALE, ADMIRED FEMALE, ADMIRED MALE) tended to be construed stereotypically.

Correlations between grid elements were examined in order to illuminate the stereotypic perceptions of males and females. Analysis revealed that homosexual males perceived VERY MASCULINE MALE as most similar to ATHLETIC PERSON ($r = .85$), and as most different than CLOSE FEMALE FRIEND ($r = -.66$), MOTHER ($r = -64$) and VERY FEMININE FEMALE ($r = -.50$). Heterosexual males also described VERY MASCULINE MALE as most similar to ATHLETIC PERSON ($r = .82$), and as contrasting with VERY FEMININE FE-MALE ($r = -.72$), CLOSE FEMALE FRIEND ($r = -.71$) and EX-SPOUSE ($r = -.60$). It is interesting to note the prominence of MOTHER in the homosexual group's perceptions of "unmasculine" figures. Both male groups perceived a set of female figures as contrasting with the VERY MASCULINE MALE, indicating a degree of sex-role stereotypic perceptions.

Examination of correlations between VERY FEMININE FEMALE and other elements revealed that both homosexual and heterosexual groups perceived her as opposite to VERY MASCULINE MALE. Homosexual males additionally characterized her as similar to MOTHER ($r = .78$) and as different than ADMIRED MALE ($r = -.73$), ADMIRED FEMALE ($r = -.72$) and IDEAL SELF ($r = -.42$). Heterosexual males described her as similar to EX-SPOUSE ($r = .80$) and CLOSE FEMALE FRIEND ($r = .66$) and as contrasting with ATHLETIC PERSON ($r = -.59$) and ADMIRED MALE ($r = -.42$). It can be seen that heterosexual males tended to perceive VERY FEMININE FEMALE stereotypically, that is, as similar to female figures and different than male figures. Homosexual males, on the other hand, evaluated her unfavorably as the polar opposite of admired figures.

Distances between paired male and female elements are presented in Table 2. It may be noted that Slater (1976, p. 62) has defined element distance measures as perceived psychological similarity between any two figures on the grid. The expected distance between any two figures may be taken as 1.

Table 2 indicates that there was a tendency for homosexual males to perceive less discrepancy between the sexes than did heterosexual

Table 2

Perceived Distances between Male and Female Elements: Male Subjects

Element Pair	Homosexual Males	Heterosexual Males
Close Female Friend - Close Male Friend	.60	.66
Admired Female - Admired Male	.37	.32
Very Feminine Female - Very Masculine Male	1.56	1.85

males, which is in agreement with the prediction that homosexual males would construe others in less sex-role stereotypic terms. As would be expected, both groups perceived a large distance between VERY MASCULINE MALE and VERY FEMININE FEMALE. Distances between the other male and female element pairs were small. Several predictions made in the present study were supported by the results. Heterosexual males did perceive other males and females in sex-role stereotypic terms, a finding consistent with previous research. Homosexual males, on the other hand, stereotyped the sexes to a markedly lesser degree. While some evidence of sex-role stereotyping was present in their descriptions of self and of other figures of both sexes, dimensions such as attractiveness and expressiveness seemed more important to their views of other people. This finding supports the prediction that homosexuals would be less likely than heterosexuals to apply stereotypic role perceptions to others.

The finding that homosexual males perceived both sexes less stereotypically than did their heterosexual counterparts could be interpreted in several ways. First, it is possible that homosexual males would tend to mix socially with fellow homosexuals, and other atypical people, who may be less bound by stereotypic roles than the acquaintances of heterosexual males.

Alternatively, if homosexual males do generally perceive people in less sex-role stereotypic terms, it may be that their personal commitment to a life outside traditional sex roles makes them reluctant to apply restrictive sex stereotypes to others. This view was presented several times to the author by homosexual males, who tended to regard sex-role stereotypes as undesirable, and tried to avoid using them when relating to other people.

Evaluation of Masculinity and Femininity

The evaluation of masculine and feminine traits by homosexual and heterosexual males was examined by studying those traits attributed to admired and to sex-role stereotypic figures. Analysis was based upon correlations greater than .6 or less than − .6 between elements and constructs. It may be noted that correlations reflect the relationships between one element and all other elements on a particular dimension, as distinct from absolute scores on that dimension. Both male groups characterized their IDEAL SELF as UNCONVENTIONAL, UNRESTRICTED, INFLUENTIAL, EXPRESSES EMOTIONS EASILY and COMPASSIONATE. In addition, homosexual males desired to be KIND, GENTLE and SPONTANEOUS, while heterosexual males wished to be INDEPENDENT. These traits comprise a mixture of socially desirable words drawn from both masculine and feminine stereotypes. In the light of previous findings (for example, Saghir & Robins, 1973; Thompson et al., 1973) that homosexual males tend to describe themselves as more feminine than do heterosexual males, interest attaches to the observation that homosexual males valued introceptive and expressive traits more highly for their ideal self.

To further illuminate the evaluation of masculinity and femininity by male subjects, correlations between admired figures and crude sex-role stereotypic figures were compared for the two male groups. Table 3 presents this information, which was derived from an *INGRID* analysis (Slater, 1976).

As can be seen from Table 3, homosexual males evaluated the VERY FEMININE FEMALE more negatively than did heterosexual males. In addition, their ideal self descriptions expressed their wish to be less similar to both sex-role stereotypic figures. Heterosexual males perceived ADMIRED MALE and ADMIRED FEMALE as less masculine than did their homosexual counterparts. They construed ADMIRED MALE as both more masculine and less feminine than ADMIRED FEMALE. Homosexual males did not distinguish the sexes in this way, indicating a less sex-role stereotypic outlook.

Table 3

Correlations between Male Subjects' Perceptions of Admired Figures and

of Sex-Role Stereotypic Figures

Element Pair	Homosexual Males	Heterosexual Males
Very Masculine Male and: Ideal Self	-.40	.00
Admired Female	-.01	-.82
Admired Male	.12	-.48
Very Feminine Female and: Ideal Self	-.42	-.27
Admired Female	-.72	-.27
Admired Male	-.74	-.42

The above result indicated that both masculine and feminine stereotypic figures were considered undesirable by present homosexual and heterosexual male subjects. Only a limited selection of stereotypic traits were attributed by these subjects to VERY MASCULINE MALE and VERY FEMININE FEMALE, and these tended to comprise the least desirable aspects of the stereotypes. Positive aspects of each stereotype were noticeably absent from descriptions. These findings were contrary to previous research concerning evaluation of masculinity and femininity. For example, Broverman, Broverman, Clarkson, Rosenkratz and Vogel (1970) and McKee and Sherriffs (1957) have suggested that both sex-role stereotypes are considered desirable for the appropriate sex, although, in an absolute sense, masculine traits are more highly valued than feminine ones. Also, Jenkin and Vroegh (1969) reported that masculinity and femininity were positively valued by both sexes, and were perceived as sharing a large number of socially desirable traits.

Of the two subject groups, only homosexual males considered androgynous traits desirable for both males and females. Heterosexual males perceived ADMIRED FEMALE in desirable feminine terms, ADMIRED MALE in different, desirable masculine terms. Homosexual males did not distinguish between admired figures in this way, but described both in similar (androgynous) terms.

Gender Identity: Descriptions of SELF and IDEAL SELF

Element distances between SELF and the remaining figures on the grid are presented in Table 4.

From Table 4, differences between homosexual and heterosexual males in terms of the perceived similarity of their SELF to each other figure may be noted. First, however, mean distances between SELF and the remaining elements were calculated for each group, in order to ensure that these differences did not result from a greater overall sense of social isolation of the part of one group. For homosexual males, mean distance between SELF and other figures was .89, for heterosexual males it was .83. From these similar results, it was concluded that the two groups could justifiably be compared on an element by element basis.

Homosexual males perceived themselves as most similar to CLOSE MALE FRIEND, BROTHER, CLOSE FEMALE FRIEND and VERY FEMININE FEMALE, and as most distant from VERY MASCULINE MALE and IDEAL SELF. Similarly, heterosexual males felt closest to CLOSE MALE FRIEND, FATHER, BROTHER, CLOSE FEMALE FRIEND and EX-SPOUSE. Most contrasting figures very VERY MASCULINE MALE and IDEAL SELF. It can be seen that neither homo-

Table 4

Distances between 'Self' and Other Elements, as Perceived by Homosexual

and Heterosexual Males

Element Distance˙	Homosexual Males	Heterosexual Males
Self and: Ideal Self	1.38	1.34
Mother	.86	.81
Father	.84	.57
Very Masculine Male	1.41	1.50
Very Feminine Female	.77	.99
Athletic Person	.92	.91
Close Male Friend	.59	.58
Close Female Friend	.68	.72
Ex-Spouse	.80	.73
Admired Female	.95	.85
Admired Male	.87	.90
Brother	.67	.62
Spouse	.84	.93

sexual nor heterosexual males perceived themselves as extremely masculine. For heterosexual males this unexpected finding may be related to the present sample's high level of education.

T-tests were carried out on mean self-ratings of each group on 14 constructs. Homosexual males perceived themselves as significantly less conventional (t (58) = 2.37, p < .05), less restricted (t (58) = 2.16, p < .05) and more passive (t (58) = 2.15, p < .05) than did their heterosexual counterparts. On the remaining 11 constructs, self-ratings of the two groups did not differ significantly. The finding that homosexual males tend to obtain higher scores than heterosexual males on scales of self-rated 'unconventionality' has been reported previously (Stringer & Grygier, 1976), and may possibly be related to the minority group status of homosexuals within our society.

Table 5 presents distances between IDEAL SELF and the remaining elements as perceived by homosexual and heterosexual males.

Mean distances between IDEAL SELF and the remaining elements on the grid were calculated for the two groups. For homosexual males, mean distance was 1.33, for heterosexual males it was 1.31. It was concluded from these similar figures that the two groups could be compared on an element by element basis.

From Table 5, it can be seen that both male groups wished to be similar to ADMIRED FEMALE and ADMIRED MALE. Heterosexuals wished to be most similar to ADMIRED MALE, homosexual to AD-MIRED FEMALE. Both groups wished to be most distant from FATHER and VERY MASCULINE MALE, with somewhat more extreme differences being desired in both instances by homosexual males.

As we noted previously, homosexual males described a more expressive, introceptive IDEAL SELF than did their heterosexual counterparts. However, differences between ideal self ratings of the two groups were slight, and significance was obtained for only three constructs. Homosexual males wished to be significantly more unconventional (t (58) = 2.63, p < .05), less active (t (58) = 2.20, p < .05) and able to express emotions more easily (t (58) = 2.66, p < .05).

The most noticeable feature of both self and ideal self ratings of male subjects was the rejection of extreme masculinity. Members of neither group perceived themselves as strongly masculine, nor did they wish to be so. Homosexual males indicated a desire to possess higher

Table 5

Distances between 'Ideal Self' and Other Elements, as Perceived by

Homosexual and Heterosexual Males

Element Distance	Homosexual Males	Heterosexual Males
Ideal Self and:		
Mother	1.62	1.37
Father	1.92	1.60
Very Masculine Male	1.84	1.58
Very Feminine Female	1.59	1.56
Athletic Person	1.50	1.34
Close Male Friend	1.16	1.33
Close Female Friend	.91	1.17
Ex-Spouse	1.26	1.56
Admired Female	.73	.82
Admired Male	.85	.73
Brother	1.44	1.57
Spouse	1.07	1.03

levels of a few feminine traits, and described themselves as slightly more similar to the VERY FEMININE FEMALE, than did heterosexual males.

Perception of Parents

In the tradition of previous research using measures of perceived similarity to investigate relationships between parents and children, distances between elements on the repertory grid were taken as measures of perceived similarity. Since no clear view emerged from the literature as to the relative importance of self and ideal self descriptions in indicating perceived relations to parents, associations were considered for SELF and IDEAL SELF separately. This method followed Ryle and Lunghi (1972).

The homosexual males were more distant from their fathers than heterosexual males. In addition, there was a tendency for heterosexual males to perceive both their SELF and their IDEAL SELF as more similar to FATHER, a finding that is consistent with many previous studies (for example, Evans, 1969; Stephan, 1973; Thompson et al., 1973). Results concerning perceptions of MOTHER were less conclusive. Both groups described SELF equally as distant from MOTHER. However, the IDEAL SELF of heterosexual males was construed as more similar to MOTHER than that of homosexual males. This finding conflicts with a number of previous studies (for example, Saghir & Robins, 1973; Stephan, 1973) which have suggested that of the two groups, homosexual males tend to describe a closer, more intense relationship with their mothers.

The present heterosexual male subjects followed the expected identification pattern of male children, with SELF being perceived as closer to FATHER than to MOTHER. Homosexual males, on the other hand, felt equally distant from both parents.

Inter-relationships between parental figures and the remaining grid elements and constructs were examined. The following characterizations are based upon correlations greater than .6 or less than − .6 except where otherwise specified.

Homosexual males perceived MOTHER as relatively DEPENDENT, INTROVERTED, PASSIVE and NOT AMBITIOUS. It can be seen that these traits constitute the ineffectual aspects of the feminine stereotype, and closely resemble those attributed to VERY FEMININE FEMALE. Heterosexual males characterized MOTHER as RESTRICTED and NOT AMBITIOUS.

MOTHER was perceived by homosexual sons as most similar to VERY FEMININE FEMALE (r = .78), and as most different than ADMIRED MALE (r = − .69), VERY MASCULINE MALE (r = − .64)

Table 6

Perceived Distances of Homosexual and Heterosexual Sons from their Parents

Element Distance		Homosexual Males	Heterosexual Males
Self	- Mother	.86	.81
Self	- Father	.84	.57
Ideal Self	- Mother	1.62	1.37
Ideal Self	- Father	1.92	1.00

and ADMIRED FEMALE ($r = -.57$). Thus MOTHER was construed both as highly feminine, and as the polar opposite of admired figures. Heterosexual males, on the other hand, perceived MOTHER as most similar to CLOSE FEMALE FRIEND ($r = .49$) and as contrasting with ADMIRED MALE ($r = -.47$), VERY MASCULINE MALE ($r = -.47$) and CLOSE MALE FRIEND ($r = -.42$).

Both male groups characterized FATHER unfavorably. In relation to other grid elements, homosexual sons described him as CONVEN-TIONAL, RESTRICTED, INTROVERTED, CONTROLLED, UNAT-TRACTIVE and NOT COMPASSIONATE. Heterosexual sons employed a similar set of traits: CONVENTIONAL, RESTRICTED, CON-TROLLED, UNATTRACTIVE and HAS TROUBLE EXPRESSING EMOTIONS. Homosexual males saw FATHER as most similar to BROTHER ($r = .32$) and as most distant from IDEAL SELF ($r = -.86$), ADMIRED FEMALE ($r = -.72$) and CLOSE FEMALE FRIEND ($r = -.60$). The high negative correlation between IDEAL SELF and FATHER strengthens the impression that homosexual males evaluated their father very negatively.

Heterosexual males perceived FATHER as closer to BROTHER ($r = .74$) and SELF ($r = .56$) and as opposite to ADMIRED FEMALE ($r = -.82$), IDEAL SELF ($r = -.75$) and SPOUSE ($r = -.70$). While heterosexual males tended to see themselves as quite similar to FATHER, the high negative correlation between IDEAL SELF and FATHER indicated rejection of him as a model.

Researchers' emphasis on the role of the family background in the etiology of homosexuality has been widely criticized by homosexuals as an outdated Freudian notion. Nevertheless, grid results indicated that homosexual males perceived SELF as more distant from FATHER than did heterosexual controls. This finding could be interpreted in several ways. Previous researchers (for example, Evans, 1969; Stephan, 1973) have concluded that fathers of homosexual males tend to reject their sons emotionally and fail to provide satisfactory male models. Alternatively, sons may reject the father as representing a heterosexual masculine role which they see as undesirable. Since fathers have been found (for example, Biller, 1971) to play a central role in the establishment of masculine gender identity in their sons, a mutual breakdown of the relationship would be a possible consequence of the son not following the pattern of heterosexual gender identity development.

To summarize these results, the father-son relationship described by male subjects followed the pattern predicted by previous research. Homosexual males tended to perceive themselves as more distant psychologically from their fathers than did heterosexual controls. Findings concerning mother-son relations were less conclusive, as would be expected from the notion (Thompson & McCandless, 1976) that fathers play a more crucial role than mothers in establishing the gender identity of their sons. Homosexual males failed to display the expected pattern of identification of male children with their fathers. Finally, both groups agreed in depicting their fathers in extremely unfavorable terms. This unexpected finding may be associated with the unusually high educational level of the present sample. Additionally, it has been reported (Thompson & McCandless, 1976) that normally adjusted adolescent children tend to reject their parents. The low mean age of the present sample may therefore be related to their tendency to reject their fathers. Rejection of fathers of a model in the homosexual group may, however, have been a function of rejection of a heterosexual male model. It cannot be determined whether the increased distance between homosexuals and their fathers was a function of increased distance because of the son's homosexuality or whether there is a causal relationship in the opposite direction. It may well be that the distance is a result of father's rejection of the unconventionality of the homosexual son. Further research will be required to elucidate this.

CONCLUSIONS

From the data, it would appear that while both homosexual and heterosexual men saw others in sex-role stereotypic terms, stereotyping was stronger in heterosexuals than homosexuals. The groups demonstrated a number of similarities in their evaluation of masculinity and femininity, although homosexual men tended to value expressive traits more highly. Of interest was the fact that masculine and feminine stereo-typic figures were considered undesirable by both groups. In terms of gender identity, descriptions of SELF and IDEAL SELF did not differ systematically between groups, and neither group saw itself as par-ticularly masculine.

Perceptions of parents indicated that both groups saw themselves as equally distant from their mothers; homosexuals were more distant from their fathers. Both groups described their fathers unfavorably, although homosexual men appeared more strongly to reject their father as a model. This could be due either to rejection of a heterosexual male model or to increased distance between father and son as a result of the son's unconventional or homosexual lifestyle.

While it is impossible to impute causality, these data demonstrate a number of similarities between homosexual and heterosexual men in terms of their perceptions of significant others.

REFERENCE NOTE

1. Elman, J. B., Press, A. and Rosenkrantz, P.S. Sex-roles and self-concept: Real and ideal. Paper presented at the meeting of the American Psychological Association, Miami, August, 1970.

REFERENCES

Bem, S. L. The measurement of psychological androgyny. *Journal of Consulting and Clinical Psychology,* 1974, *42*, 152-162.

Bene, E. On the genesis of male homosexuality: An attempt at clarifying the role of the parents. *British Journal of Psychiatry,* 1965, *111*, 803-813.

Bernard, L. C. and Epstein, D. J. Androgyny scores of matched homosexual and heterosexual males. *Journal of Homosexuality,* 1978, *4*, 169-178.

Biller, H. B. *Father, child and sex-role.* Lexington, MA: D.C. Heath, 1971.

Broverman, I. K., Broverman, D. M., Clarkson, F. E., Rosenkratz, P. and Vogel, S. R. Sex-role stereotypes and clinical judgment of mental health. *Journal of Consulting Psychology,* 1970, *34*, 1-7.

Chang, J. and Block, J. A study of male homosexuals. *Journal of Consulting Psychology,* 1960, *24*, 307-310.

Evans, R. Childhood parental relationships of homosexual men. *Journal of Consulting and Clinical Psychology,* 1969, *33*, 129-135.

Fransella, F. and Bannister, D. *A manual for repertory grid technique.* London: Academic Press, 1977.

Greenblatt, D. R. Semantic differential analysis of the "triangular system" hypothesis in "adjusted" male homosexuals. (Doctoral dissertation, University of California, Los Angeles, 1966). *Dissertation Abstracts International,* 1967, 27(B), 4123-4124.

Hooberman, R. E. Gender identity and gender role of male homosexuals and heterosexuals. (Doctoral dissertation, University of Michigan, 1975.) *Dissertation Abstracts International,* April 1976, *36* (10A), 6554.

Jenkin, N. and Vroegh, K. Contemporary concepts of masculinity and femininity. *Psychological Reports,* 1969, *25*, 679-697.

Kelly, G. A. *The psychology of personal constructs* (Vols. 1 & 2). New York: Norton, 1955.

Kinsey, A. C., Pomeroy, W. B. and Martin, C. F. *Sexual behavior in the human male.* Phila-delphia: W.B. Saunders, 1948.

Lunneborg, P. W. Stereotypic aspects in masculinity-femininity measurement. *Journal of Consulting and Clinical Psychology,* 1970, *34,* 113-118.

McKee, J. P. and Sherriffs, A. C. The differential evaluation of males and females. *Journal of Personality,* 1957, *25,* 356-371.

Ryle, A. and Lunghi, M. Parental and sex role identification of students measured with a repertory grid technique. *British Journal of Social and Clinical Psychology,* 1972, *11,* 149-161.

Saghir, M. T. and Robins, E. *Male and female homosexuality: A comprehensive investigation.* Baltimore: Williams & Wilkins, 1973.

Schofield, M. *Sociological aspects of homosexuality: A comparative study of three types of homosexuals.* Boston: Little, Brown, 1965.

Siegelman, M. Parental background of male homosexuals and heterosexuals. *Archives of Sexual Behavior,* 1974, *3,* 3-18.

Slater, P. (Ed.). *The measurement of interpersonal space by grid technique* (Vol. 2). London: Wiley, 1972.

Stephan, W. G. Parental relationships and early social experiences of activist male homosexuals and heterosexuals. *Journal of Abnormal Psychology,* 1973, *82,* 506-513.

Stringer, P. and Grygier, T. Male homosexuality, psychiatric patient status, and psychological masculinity and femininity. *Archives of Sexual Behavior,* 1976, *5*(1), 15-287.

Thompson, N. L. and McCandless, B. The homosexual orientation and its antecedents. In A. Davids (Ed.), *Child personality and psychopathology: Current topics* (Vol. 3). New York: Wiley, 1976.

Thompson, N. L., Schwartz, D. M., McCandless, B. R. and Edwards, D. A. Parent-child relationships and sexual identity in male and female homosexuals and heterosexuals. *Journal of Consulting and Clinical Psychology,* 1973, *41,* 120-127.

West, D. J. *Homosexuality re-examined.* London: Duckworth, 1977.

Parental and Interpersonal Relationships of Transsexual and Masculine and Feminine Homosexual Men

Iva Šípová, PhD
Antonin Brzek, MD
Charles University

ABSTRACT. A group of transsexual and homosexual men was examined using the Leary Test as a psycho-sociogram, and findings were compared to those from a group of heterosexual men. It was found that the fathers of homosexuals and transsexuals were more hostile and less dominant than the fathers of the control group and hence less desirable identification models. The average mothers of transsexuals were close to the ideal person in our culture, e.g., dominant, strong and kindly, and thus an imposing identification model.

Heterosexual men and transsexuals, in their behavior towards their wives, on the average identified with the models set by their fathers. Effeminate homosexuals in relations towards their male partners on the average identified with their mothers. Non-effeminate homosexuals modeled their behavior somewhere between both parents.

Heterosexual men tended to choose wives modelled on their mothers and modelled their behavior towards their wives on their fathers' behavior. Non-effeminate homosexuals tended to choose their male partners according to the model set by their mothers and behaved toward them in a more dominant manner than any of the other groups studied (effeminate homosexuals, non-effeminate homosexuals and transsexuals). Effeminate homosexuals on average chose the most dominant male partners and modelled their behavior toward them on that of their mothers. The wives of transsexuals were rated as the most hostile.

The self-esteem of all the groups studied suffered from lack of dominance. On the average, non-effeminate homosexuals were found to be closest to the heterosexual norms, transsexuals the furthest.

INTRODUCTION

Homosexuals and transsexuals who sought out the help of the Institute of Sexology very often reported disturbed relationships between the parents and between parents and the patients. This clinical impres-

---

Both authors are from the Institute of Sexology, Charles University, Karlovo nám. 32, 121 11 Praha 2, Czechoslovakia.

© 1983 by The Haworth Press, Inc. All rights reserved.

sion was confirmed by the evaluation of a sample of family case histories (Šípová, 1976). In the present study we attempted to test the hypothesis that there is a deformation of relationships in the families of effeminate and non-effeminate homosexuals and transsexuals who present as patients.

SUBJECTS AND METHODS

Twenty-seven transsexual (male-to-female) men with an average age of 27 years, 100 effeminate homosexual men with average age of 22.9 years and 70 non-effeminate homosexual men with an average age of 26.3 years were examined by the Leary Personality and Interpersonal Relations Test (Leary, Note 1, 1957), which was used as a psychosociogram using the approach of Mellan (1966). Leary based his evaluation of personality and interpersonal behavior on two polar principals: dominance-submission, love-hostility. He expressed them in a graphic form of co-ordinates, where the vertical axis represents the continuum of dominance-submission and the horizontal axis the love-hostility continuum. Subjects fill out a 128-item questionnaire, which is evaluated and the "center of gravity of a personalty" is determined. If the Leary Test is used as a sociogram (Mellan, 1966), the relationships of persons evaluated in these two polar dimensions may be assessed in the way in which the subject sees them. The findings were compared to a sample of 41 heterosexual men with an average age of 30.7 years who had presented to the Sexology Clinic because of the infertility of their marriages and whose andrological examination, including a spermiogram, was found to be well within standard limits. The homosexuals were placed in effeminate and non-effeminate groups on the basis of an interview carried out by a psychologist—one of the present authors. The psychologist based her estimation on social behavior of a patient during the interview, on his clothing, and mainly on the preference for either a feminine or a masculine role during intercourse as reported by the patient himself. All the respondents were patients of the Sexological Institute, whose professionals they contacted because of their problems.

Each man was asked to describe himself, the father and mother (or possibly foster-father or foster-mother) with whom he lived since childhood and also to assess his sexual partners, if he had them. He was also asked to rate how he assumed he would be assessed by his partners. We determined arithmetic means and standard deviations of the examined groups on indices of dominance and love according to Leary. The Smirnov-Kolmogorov Test was used to determine statistical sig-

nificance. The Pearson Test (2 × 2) was used in the group of transsexuals as this group was small in number.

FINDINGS

The mean values of dominance and love in self-assessments, the assessments of fathers, assessments of mothers and assessments of male
or female partners and assumed assessments of self by partner in each
of the groups studies (including the control group) appear in Table 1.

Assessment of Parents (Figure 1)

Among the average fathers of all the experimental groups (homosexuals and transsexuals) there is less dominance and more hostility
reported than in the control group. In particular, the average father
of the effeminate homosexual is reported to be harsh and selfish. The
average father of the transsexual is reported to be hostile, but at the
same time not very dominant. The average mothers of all the studied
groups are reported to be less kind: the least kind is the average mother
of the non-effeminate homosexual who is also the least dominant. The
most dominant of all is the average mother of the transsexual, who is
reported to be supernormally strong.

In the paternal relationships of men in the control group, respondents
get on well with their fathers because they were reported to be tolerant.
The paternal relationships of the fathers of effeminate homosexuals are
reportedly marked by the father's harshness and lack of kindness, which
are a source of suffering for the child. Among the parents of non-
effeminate homosexuals there is comparatively little kindness or useful
authority reported, while the realtionships between the average parents
of transsexuals and their children show a maternal dominance.

Self-Assessment and Identification (Figure 2)

The men in the control group rated themselves on the average as
moderately dominant and moderately kind. In the presumed assessment
by their wives, there was more dominance, and also a markedly strong
identification with fathers. In comparison to the control group this difference is statistically significant at the 1% level (Table 2). The group
of non-effeminate homosexuals comes closest to the control group in
this respect and conversely, the transsexual group was found to be most
passive and dependent. In the average self-assessment of the studied
groups there is a very marked decline in dominance in relation to both
parents (Tables 3 and 4). The transsexual group did not have any male
partners (only a desire for them). Five of the transsexuals were married.

TABLE 1

AVERAGE VALUES OF DOMINANCE AND LOVE IN SELF-ASSESSMENT, ASSESSMENT OF FATHER, ASSESSMENT OF MOTHER, ASSESSMENT OF PARTNER AND ASSUMED ASSESSMENT BY PARTNER

			SELF-ASSESSMENT		ASSESSMENT OF FATHER		ASSESSMENT OF MOTHER		ASSESSMENT OF PARTNER		ASSUMED ASSESSMENT BY PARTNER	
	N		D	L	D	L	D	L	D	L	D	L
Control men	41	x	3.4	3.6	6.5	1.9	2.4	8.4	2.9	6.1	6.0	3.1
		s	5.9	7.0	8.7	8.5	6.9	10.7	6.3	9.6	7.1	8.0
Non-effeminate homosexual men	70	x	-1.6	2.9	4.2	-0.1	0.0	3.1	1.8	4.0	3.8	3.4
		s	7.6	8.9	8.1	12.3	7.4	11.0	6.6	9.0	7.6	10.4
Effeminate homosexual men	100	x	-4.3	6.2	5.4	-1.8	2.4	8.3	4.7	4.3	1.3	5.5
		s	9.2	9.8	7.9	10.7	6.7	10.9	7.9	8.6	8.4	10.1
Transsexual men	27	x	-6.4	5.9	3.3	-1.2	5.1	3.7	2.4	1.0	1.4	-2.9
		s	9.2	9.1	5.7	9.2	8.2	11.5	5.9	6.5	6.1	4.3

N = number of persons in sample
x = standard deviation
s = standard deviation
D = dominance index in Leary Test
L - love index in Leary Test

Figure 1
Assessment of parents and their relationships

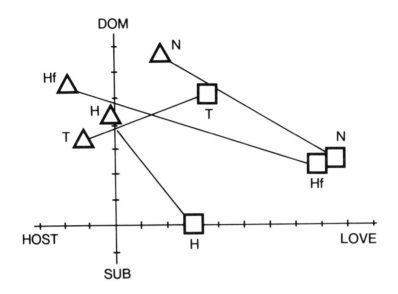

Average Assessment of

△ N = Fathers of control men
□ N = Mothers " " "

△ H = Fathers of non-effeminate homosexuals
□ H = Mothers " • " "

△ Hf = Fathers of effeminate homosexuals
□ Hf = Mothers • " "

△ T = Fathers of transsexuals
□ T = Mothers • "

Their behavior towards their wives was, on the average, hostile and non-dominant, and there was some indication of identification with fathers. The behavior of non-effeminate homosexuals towards their male partners lies somewhere between that of their fathers and mothers and in this respect their scores approach the scores obtained from the control group of heterosexual men.

Figure 2
Self-assessment and identification

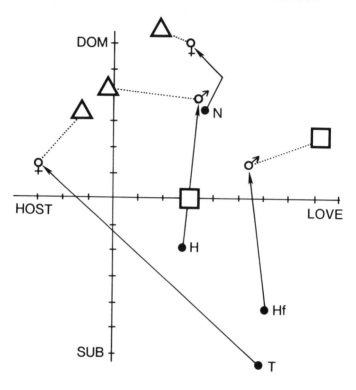

△ = Average father

□ = Average mother

···· = Identification

● = Self assessment

♂ = Assumed assessment by male partner

♀ =   "   "   "   wife

N = Men of control group

H = Non-effeminate homosexual men

Hf = Effeminate homosexual men

T   = Transsexual men

TABLE 2

DIFFERENCES IN SELF-ASSESSED AVERAGE DOMINANCE BETWEEN CONTROL MEN

AND HOMOSEXUAL AND TRANSSEXUAL GROUPS

	AVERAGE DOMINANCE	SIGNIFICANCE
Control men	+ 3.4	
Non-effeminate homosexual men	- 1.6	1%
Effeminate homosexual men	- 4.3	1%
Transsexual men	- 6.4	0.5%

Behavior towards Partners: Comparison with Parents (Figure 3)

The control (heterosexual) group was found to have chosen a wife modeled on their mother. In addition, the average male partner of a non-effeminate homosexual was found to be similar to the non-effeminate homosexual's mother. The average male partner of effeminate homosexuals was also found to be closer to his mother than to his father, but at the same time this group has the highest reported partner dominance of all the studied groups. The wife of a transsexual is somewhere between the transsexual's mother and father, has the highest dominance of all the average partners and is the most hostile.

DISCUSSION AND CONCLUSIONS

Recent research has called attention to the significance of paternal care and the importance of emotional contacts between father and child for developing the personality of the child. Lynn (1969, 1974) has stressed that a boy who strongly identifies with a father and especially with a father who has marked male characteristics, does not suffer from anxiety. Our control group has reported kind, caring and at the same time vigorous fathers endowed with authority. They appear to represent desirable identification models for their sons also in relation to women. It was found that our control group of heterosexual men strongly identified themselves with their fathers, as far as their socio-sexual behavior was concerned. Within their own marriages they had accepted the model of the relationship that had existed between their parents and they chose wives predominantly modeled on their mothers.

TABLE 3

DIFFERENCES IN SELF-ASSESSED AVERAGE DOMINANCE

AND ASSESSED AVERAGE DOMINANCE IN FATHERS

	AVERAGE DOMINANCE IN SELF-ASSESSMENT	AVERAGE DOMINANCE OF FATHERS	SIGNIFICANCE
Control men	+ 3.4	+ 6.5	n.s.
Non-effeminate homosexual men	- 1.6	+ 4.2	1%
Effeminate homosexual men	- 4.3	+ 5.4	1%
Transsexual men	- 6.4	+ 3.3	0.5%

TABLE 4

DIFFERENCES IN SELF-ASSESSED AVERAGE DOMINANCE

AND ASSESSED AVERAGE DOMINANCE OF MOTHERS

	AVERAGE DOMINANCE IN SELF-ASSESSMENT	AVERAGE DOMINANCE OF MOTHERS	SIGNIFICANCE
Control men	+ 3.4	+ 2.4	n.s.
Non-effeminate homosexual men	- 1.6	+ 0.0	1%
Effeminate homosexual men	- 4.3	+ 2.4	1%
Transsexual men	- 6.4	+ 5.1	0.5%

The fathers of homosexuals and transsexuals in our study were on the average reportedly more hostile and less dominant. As identification models they ranged from not very desirable to highly unsatisfactory. In particular, the fathers of effeminate homosexuals were frequently reported as uncaring, unkind and harsh. Their sons appeared to become emotionally attached to their mothers, who often tended to protect them against their fathers. In relations with their partners, the effeminate homosexuals then tended to identify with their mothers, to behave in an effeminate manner and on the average to choose partners who were dominant and kind. The fathers of transsexuals are frequently not only hostile and uncaring, but also not very dominant. In a marriage with a strong and domiant mother, they are unimposing. The majority of our group of transsexuals did not have any relationship with a man, which they longed to form. As a consequence such a relationship could not be assessed. Those who were married, had on the average, the least kind partners when compared to the male partners of homosexuals and the wives of the men in the control group, and they behaved towards them in a hostile and non-dominating manner. Thus in their relation-

Figure 3
Behaviour towards partners:
Comparison with parents

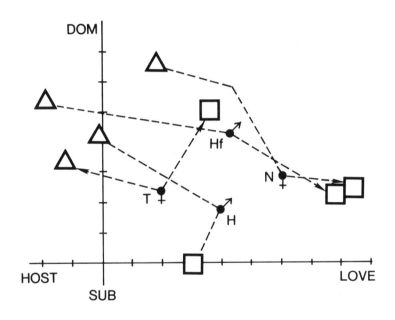

△	= Average father
□	= " mother
♀ N =	" wife of control men
♀ T =	" wife of transsexual men
♂ H =	" male partner of non-effeminate homosexual men
♂ Hf =	" male partner of effeminate homosexual men

ships towards women, they tended to identify with their fathers. The socio-sexual identification of non-effeminate homosexuals on the average lay between both parents and they tended to choose partners who were similar to their mothers; their average behavior towards the partners was most masculine when compared to the other studied groups (transsexuals and effeminate homosexuals).

Medinus (1955), Lynn and Sawrey (1959) and Coopersmith (1967) have pointed out that the development of self-esteem in boys is directly dependent on the degree to which the father was committed to their rearing and the strength of the emotional bond with him. The homosexuals and transsexuals in our study manifested self-esteem disorders. On the basis of their own assessment they differ from both their parents by their submissiveness, passivity and dependency. Non-effeminate homosexuals are closest to standard behavior and their average father is also closest to the average father in the control group. Transsexuals are most deviant and their average father is furthest away from the average father of the control group. It thus seems that our findings confirm the findings of these authors.

On the other hand, we are aware of the fact that androgens contribute to such qualities as being energetic and vigorous, as well as to hostility. Eunuchoids are extremely passive and submissive, as well as extremely kind. Self-assessment in which there is marked lack of so-called masculine characteristics may also be connected with a lack of androgens. Previously Starka, Šípová and Hynie (1975) have been able to determine somewhat lower levels of androgens in transsexuals and homosexuals that were in accord with the findings of psychosocial examination. Transsexuals had the lowest androgen levels, followed by effeminate homosexuals. Non-effeminate homosexuals most closely approached the level achieved by a control group. Hence we concluded that the degree of androgen supply might also contribute to the multifactorial genesis of gender identity disorders, influence the extent of the disorder, and contribute to differences in the self-assessment of these people.

Šípová (1976) has also shown, on the basis of case histories, the frequent absence of fathers or existence of a disharmonious family environment among men with gender identity disorders. It thus seems to us than an unimposing paternal identification model should be included among the significant psychogenic factors of these conditions, at least in the clinical population studied.

REFERENCE NOTE

1. Leary, T. *Multilevel measurement of interpersonal behavior: A manual for the use of interpersonal systems of Personality*. Psychological Consultation Service. Berkeley, CA, 1956.

REFERENCES

Coopersmith, S. *The antecedents of self-esteem.* San Francisco: W. H. Freeman, 1967.

Leary, T. *Interpersonal diagnosis of personality.* New York: The Ronald Press, 1957.

Lynn, D. B. *Parental and sex-role identification.* Berkeley: McCutchan, 1969.

Lynn, D. B. *The father, his role in child development.* Monterey, CA: Brooks-Cole Publishing Company, 1974.

Lynn, D. B. & Sawrey, W. L. The effects of father-absence on Norwegian boys and girls. *Journal of Abnormal and Social Psychology,* 1959, *59*, 258-262.

Medinus, G. R. Adolescent self-acceptance and perceptions of their parents. *Journal of Consulting Psychology,* 1955, *29*, 150-154.

Mellan, J. Jednoduchy zpusob administrace Learyho metody. A simple method for administering the Leary Test. *Czechoslovak Psychology,* 1966, *9*, 513-519.

Starka, L., Šípová, I. & Hynie, J. Plasma testosterone in male transsexuals and homosexuals. *Journal of Sex Research,* 1975, *11*, 134-138.

Šípová, I. Rodinne prostredi intersexualnich lidi. The family environment of intersexual persons. *Czechoslovak Pediatrics,* 1976, *31*, 629-631.

Psychological Characteristics of Bisexual, Heterosexual and Homosexual Women

Ronald A. LaTorre, PhD
University of British Columbia

Kristina Wendenburg, BA
Ministry of Human Resources, British Columbia

ABSTRACT. One hundred and twenty-five female volunteers completed a questionnaire designed to measure masculinity, femininity, body cathexis, and self-esteem. Women were categorized as bisexual, heterosexual or homosexual according to self-labeling and according to erotic preference. The proportion of androgynous and undifferentiated individuals was much greater among self-labeled homosexual women. Feminine individuals were conspicuously under-represented among self-labeled homosexual and bisexual women. Women who reported both opposite-sex and same-sex sexual experiences, regardless of their self-label or erotic preference, were more agentic (i.e., possessed more socially desirable masculine traits), more satisfied with their bodies and its functions, more satisfied with both their sexual activities and their biological sex, and more satisfied with themselves and their abilities than were women who only reported opposite-sex sexual experiences.

Classical theories of homosexuality have linked it to an inversion of gender role orientation (Ellis, 1901/1915; Freud, 1922/1959; Krafft-Ebing, 1886/1965). Freud, for example, maintained that unresolved penis envy in the girl caused her to manifest homosexuality and to exhibit masculine traits in adolescence and adulthood. Studies involving male homosexuals (who were prisoners or psychiatric patients) have substantiated those early theories (Buhrich & McConaghy, 1979; Freund, Langevin, Laws, & Serber, 1974).

More recently, theorists have suggested that the only psychological

Ronald A. LaTorre is research associate for the Vancouver School Board, sessional instructor in Psychology at the University of British Columbia, and consultant to Forensic Psychiatric Services, British Columbia Ministry of Health. Kristina Wendenburg is a child care worker for the British Columbia Ministry of Human Resources' Special Services to Children Program, and consultant for the South Okanagan Women in Need Society.

© 1983 by The Haworth Press, Inc. All rights reserved.

87

difference between homosexuals and heterosexuals was their erotic orientation. Storms (1980), using an androgyny scale (one that assesses masculinity and femininity independently), found no significant differences in the masculinity or femininity of heterosexuals, bisexuals, or homosexuals with men's and women's scores analyzed separately. Storms' findings refute those reported by Hooberman (1979) who found homosexual men to be less masculine and more feminine, and those reported by Oberstone and Sukoneck (1976) who found lesbians to be more masculine and less feminine. Theories seem to have come full circle, however; some now propose that, because of the greater incidence of androgyny (possession of gender-role traits of both sexes), homosexuals are probably better adjusted than are heterosexuals. The greater androgyny of homosexual men and women has received some empirical support (Brooks, 1981; Hooberman, 1979). Studies of nonpatient homosexual women typically show that these women have no more psychopathology than do heterosexual control women and, in some cases, attain scores indicative of better adjustment (Brooks, 1981; Oberstone & Sukoneck, 1976; Reiss, Safer, & Yotive, 1974; Siegelman, 1979).

Self-esteem is an indirect measure of psychological adjustment and it has been shown to correlate with both masculinity and, to a lesser degree, femininity (Hooberman, 1979; Spence, Helmreich & Stapp, 1975). Mucklow and Phelan (1979) as well as Strassberg, Roback, Cunningham, McKee, and Larson (1979) found no significant differences in the self-concept of heterosexual and homosexual women although Dailey (1979) reported a "clinically" impaired level of self-esteem in five lesbian couples.

The purpose of this report is to determine the masculinity, femininity, and self-esteem of bisexual, heterosexual and homosexual women. Because self-esteem is linked to body satisfaction and because one's body is of primary importance in erotic orientation, body cathexis is also assessed in this study. Specific analysis of the groups' satisfaction with sexual activities and with biological sex is also conducted.

Four analyses were conducted for each set of data. In half of the analyses, groups are determined by self-labels. That is, a person is "grouped" according to her response to the question "Do you consider yourself a homosexual. . . . bisexual. . . . or heterosexual?" While self-labeling is a frequent research criterion for group inclusion, Blumstein and Schwartz (1977) have outlined various problems with it (e.g., some individuals with extensive homosexual involvement do not label themselves homosexual while others with exclusive heterosexual involvement do). Therefore, analyses were reconducted with the criterion for group inclusion being respondents' answers to "What do you prefer? Sex with a man. . . . Sex with a woman. . . . No preference?" This is the criterion of erotic preference.

Another concern is the possible confounding of results due to variables not directly related to the grouping variable. Brooks (1981), for example, has noted that heterosexual groups have included married women. Research indicates that married women are more passive, phobic, dependent, and psychopathological. To address this issue of confounding, half of the analyses in this report are conducted on the complete sample of female volunteers and the remainder of the analyses are conducted on a "cleaner" sample of volunteers. For this smaller sample, married women, women who had not experienced coitus, and women who had not had a sexual experience with another woman were excluded. This is, according to the authors' knowledge, the only research involving homosexual women to insure that all groups had had both heterosexual and homosexual experiences. Labeling and preference should, therefore, be more valid criteria because important background differences, outside of labeling and erotic preference, are controlled.

METHOD

Procedure

Women were recruited from the Women's Center and four psychology courses (psychology of women, behavior disorders, psychology of ageing—evening course, behavior dynamics—evening course) at the University of British Columbia. One hundred and thirty women volunteered to complete the four-page questionnaire; five were subsequently excluded as a result of missing data.

Volunteers

Of the 125 volunteers who provided completed surveys, 85 labeled themselves as heterosexual, 22 labeled themselves as bisexual, and 18 labeled themselves as lesbian or homosexual. In the self-labeled heterosexual groups, 77 (90.6%) preferred sex with a man, 3 preferred sex with a woman, and 5 had no preference. Seventeen (94.4%) of the self-labeled lesbians preferred sex with a woman and 1 had no preference. Eighteen (81.8%) of self-labeled bisexuals had no preference for sex of partner in sexual activities and 4 preferred men. The percentage of agreement between self-labeling and sexual preference was 89.6%. Because self-labeling is not consistent with sexual preference, this report provides analyses of results for groups determined by self-labeling and groups determined by erotic preference.

Chi-square analyses were conducted to determine differences among the groups in marital status, coital experience and sexual experiences with women. All volunteers reported some type of sexual experience with men.

For self-labeled groups, there was no significant difference in coital experience (10.6% of heterosexual and 5.6% of homosexual women had never engaged in coitus), or in marital status (23.5% of heterosexuals were married and 18.2% of bisexuals were married). There was a significant difference (χ^2 (2) $= 57.1, p < .0001$) in their experience with female sexual partners (15.3% of heterosexual, 68.2% of bisexual, and all the homosexual women had had a sexual experience with another woman). Similarly, when groups were determined by erotic preference, no significant difference existed for coital experience (11.1% of those preferring men had not had coitus, 5.0% of those preferring women had not had coitus) or for marital status (23.5% of those preferring men were married, and 20.8% of those with no preference were married). There was a significant difference in reports of sexual experiences with other women (16.0% of those preferring men, 62.5% of those with no preference, and 90.0% of those preferring women had had a sexual experience with another woman), χ^2 (2) $= 46.2, p < .0001$.

A one-way analysis of variance with a subsequent Scheffé multiple range test were used to assess age differences among the groups. Self-labeled heterosexual women were significantly younger ($\bar{x} = 24.1$ years) than self-labeled homosexual women ($\bar{x} = 29.3$ years), $F(2,122) = 6.0, p < .005$. Average age of the self-labeled bisexuals was 26.4 years. There was no significant difference in age among groups determined by erotic preference. The average age of all respondents was 25.2 years.

Tests

The survey consisted of three psychological tests, the Extended Personal Attributes Questionnaire (EPAQ), the Body-Cathexis Scale (BC Scale), and the Rosenberg Self-Esteem Inventory, which were followed by questions soliciting general and sexual background information.

The EPAQ is a combination of the original Personality Attributes Questionnaire developed by Spence et al. (1975) and two additional scales more recently developed by Spence, Helmreich, and Holohan (1979). It consists of (a) separate Masculinity and Femininity scales containing eight socially *desirable* agentic traits (M+) and eight socially *desirable* communal traits (F+), respectively, and (b) separate Masculinity and Femininity scales containing eight socially *undesirable* agentic traits (M−) and eight socially *undesirable* communal traits (F−), respectively. The volunteers rated each trait on a 5-point scale ranging from 0 ("not at all characteristic of me") to 4 ("very characteristic of me"). The scores for each scale were summed and then divided by eight to produce a range of scores between 0 and 4 for each scale.

The BC Scale (Secord & Jourard, 1953) measures the degree of satisfaction or dissatisfaction a respondent has with her body or body functions. It consists of 46 body parts and functions that are rated on a 5-point scale from 1 ("have strong feelings and wish change could somehow be made") to 5 ("consider myself fortunate"). The total score was summed and then divided by the total number of items to produce a range of scores between 1 and 5.

On the Rosenberg Self-Esteem Scale (Rosenberg, 1965), respondents note their agreement or disagreement with each of ten statements. Scores on this test range from 0 (high self-esteem) to 6 (low self-esteem).

RESULTS

Masculinity-Femininity

One-way analyses of variance failed to demonstrate significant effects for both self-labeled and erotic-preference groupings on $M+$, $M-$, $F+$ and $F-$. Cell means and standard deviations for $M+$, $M-$, $F+$ and $F-$ are shown in Table 1. Previous sexual experience with another woman was associated with significantly elevated $M+$ scores ($\bar{x} = 2.85 \pm .45$ vs. $2.65 \pm .57$), $F(1,123) = 3.9$, $p < .05$; but marital status and coital experience were not associated with either the socially desirable or undesirable scales of masculinity and femininity. Subsequent analyses excluded married individuals, those without coital experience, and those without sexual experiences with another woman. The results were similar to those for the entire sample.

In line with the Spence et al. (1975) method of assessing androgyny, medians were determined for the $M+$ and $F+$ scales. These wre 2.75 and 3.05, respectively. Individuals scoring above the median on both scales were labeled androgynous, those scoring above the median on the $M+$ scale and below the median on the $F+$ scale were labeled masculine, those scoring below the median on the $M+$ scale and above the median on the $F+$ scale were labeled feminine, and those scoring below the median on both scales were labeled undifferentiated. The results for groups determined by self-labeling and by erotic preference are shown in Table 2. Chi-square analyses showed the distribution for self-labeled groups to be significantly different but the same was not true for groups determined by erotic preference, $\chi^2(6) = 13.9$, $p < .05$ and $\chi^2(6) = 7.7$, n.s. Among the self-labeled groups (a) gender-role categories were evenly represented for heterosexual women, (b) there was an over-representation of masculine bisexual women, (c) there was an under-representation of masculine and an over-representation of undifferentiated homosexual women, and (d) there was an under-representation of feminine bisexual and feminine homosexual women.

TABLE I

CELL MEANS AND STANDARD DEVIATIONS OF SOCIALLY DESIRABLE AND UNDESIRABLE MASCULINITY AND FEMININITY, BODY CATHEXIS, SATISFACTION WITH SEXUAL ACTIVITIES AND BIOLOGICAL SEX AND SELF-ESTEEM

| Groups | Groups Determined by | |
	Self-Labeling	Sexual Preference
Socially Desirable Masculinity (M+)		
Heterosexual	2.7	2.7
	(0.6)	(0.5)
Bisexual	2.9	2.9
	(0.5)	(0.6)
Homosexual	2.7	2.7
	(0.3)	(0.4)
Socially Undesirable Masculinity (M−)		
Heterosexual	1.1	1.2
	(0.6)	(0.6)
Bisexual	1.5	1.4
	(0.7)	(0.7)
Homosexual	1.1	1.1
	(0.4)	(0.4)
Socially Desirable Femininity (F+)		
Heterosexual	3.1	3.1
	(0.4)	(0.5)
Bisexual	2.9	2.9
	(0.5)	(0.4)
Homosexual	3.1	3.1
	(0.6)	(0.6)
Socially Undesirable Femininity (F−)		
Heterosexual	1.1	1.2
	(0.5)	(0.5)
Bisexual	0.9	0.9
	(0.5)	(0.5)
Homosexual	1.1	1.1
	(0.6)	(0.5)
Body Cathexis		
Heterosexual	3.5	3.6
	(0.4)	(0.4)
Bisexual	3.6	3.6
	(0.4)	(0.4)
Homosexual	3.7	3.7
	(0.4)	(0.5)

TABLE I (cont'd.)

Groups	Groups Determined by	
	Self-Labeling	Sexual Preference
	Satisfaction with Sexual Activities	
Heterosexual	3.9	3.9
	(1.1)	(1.0)
Bisexual	3.9	3.9
	(1.4)	(1.4)
Homosexual	3.9	4.0
	(1.2)	(1.2)
	Satisfaction with Biological Sex	
Heterosexual	4.3	4.3
	(0.6)	(0.6)
Bisexual	4.5	4.5
	(0.7)	(0.7)
Homosexual	4.6	4.6
	(0.7)	(0.7)
	Self-Esteem	
Heterosexual	1.2	1.2
	(1.1)	(1.0)
Bisexual	1.2	1.2
	(1.5)	(1.5)
Homosexual	1.1	1.1
	(1.1)	(1.3)

Body Cathexis

One-way analyses of variance conducted on body cathexis scores also failed to detect significant differences for both the self-labeled and erotic preference groupings (see Table 1). Those women who had had a sexual experience with another woman reported greater satisfaction with their bodies and body functions ($\bar{x} = 3.71 \pm .40$) than did women who had not had such a sexual experience ($\bar{x} = 3.51 \pm .40$), $F(1,123) = 6.5, p < .02$. Marital status and coital experience were not associated with differences in body cathexis. Subsequent analyses, excluding subjects who were married, who had never had coitus or who had never had sex with another woman, produced results similar to those for the entire sample.

Specific analyses were conducted for two items on the BC Scale—satisfaction with one's sexual activities and satisfaction with one's biological sex (see Table 1). The only significant effect was on the rating of satisfaction with biological sex for self-labeled groups $F(2,122) = 3.1, p < .05$. It appears from Table 1 that bisexual and homosexual

TABLE II

PERCENTAGE OF VOLUNTEERS CLASSIFIED AS ANDROGYNOUS,
MASCULINE, FEMININE OR UNDIFFERENTIATED BY
EACH GROUP CRITERION

| Groups | Gender Role Category | | | |
	Androgynous	Masculine	Feminine	Undifferentiated
	Self-Labeled Groups			
Heterosexual (n=85)	28.2	21.2	25.9	24.7
Bisexual (n=22)	31.8	36.4	0.0	31.8
Homosexual (n=18)	38.9	11.1	5.6	44.4
	Erotic Preference Groups			
Heterosexual (n=81)	28.4	22.2	23.5	25.9
Bisexual (n=24)	29.2	33.3	8.3	29.2
Homosexual (n=20)	40.0	10.0	10.0	40.0

women reported greater satisfaction with being a woman; however, a Scheffé multiple range test did not demonstrate significant group differences.

Women who had had sexual experiences with other women were more satisfied with both their sexual activities ($\bar{x}$ = 4.2 ± 1.07 vs. 3.8 ± 1.13) and their biological sex ($\bar{x}$ = 4.7 ± .56 vs. 4.2. ± .64), $F(1,123)$ = 5.2, $p < .05$ and $F(1,123)$ = 18.1, $p < .0001$, respectively. Those who had coital experience were also more satisfied with their sexual activities ($\bar{x}$ = 4.0 ± 1.09 vs. 3.1 ± 1.20) and their biological sex ($\bar{x}$ = 4.4 ± .65 vs. 3.9 ± .57) $F(1,123)$ = 6.2, $p < .02$ and $F(1,123)$ = 5.8, $p < .02$, respectively. Marital status produced no significant effect. Excluding married women, those without coital experience and those without sexual experience with another woman, no significant effects occurred regardless of groups being determined by self-labeling or erotic preference.

Self-Esteem

One-way analyses of variance again failed to detect significant differences in self-esteem among groups regardless of the criterion for grouping (see Table 1). Those reporting sexual experiences with women reported greater self-esteem ($\bar{x}$ = 0.91 ± 1.03 vs. 1.35 ± 1.24), $F(1,123)$ = 4.2, $p < .05$. Marital status and coital experience had no impact on self-esteem scores. Subsequent analyses conducted on single, coitally experienced women who had had a sexual experience with another woman produced results similar to those for the overall sample.

DISCUSSION

The research reported in this paper is, methodologically, a major step for research in female homosexuality. It defines groups according to both erotic preference and self-labels and it defines "cleaner" groups by teasing out bisexuals who have, all too often, contaminated homosexual samples.

The results of the study echo Kingdon's (1979) conclusions: with the exception of erotic preference, homosexual women possess the same psychological characteristics as do heterosexual woman. To this we can add that, with the exception of a lack of erotic preference, bisexual women display the same psychological characteristics as do heterosexual and homosexual women. The only exception is the relationship between—not overall levels of—masculinity and femininity. It is relatively uncommon to find a bisexual or homosexual woman whose femininity far exceeds her masculinity. Only 1 of 40 self-labeled homosexual and bisexual women were "feminine". Spence and Helmreich (1978) also reported that the feminine category was the least often observed among lesbians. Although there was a greater proportion of masculine lesbians in their lesbian sample, their sample may have included many who were really bisexual (MacDonald, 1981). Homosexual women tended to gravitate toward the extremes of androgyny and undifferentiation. This balance of masculinity and femininity, regardless of overall level of traits, was the original definition of androgyny (Bem, 1974) and was apparently the definition used in previous studies showing a greater incidence of androgyny among lesbians (Brooks, 1981).

Unmitigated agency (i.e., masculinity) may be actively avoided by many lesbians to avoid being labeled as "bull" or "butch"—to avoid falling prey to the stereotype of a virago. The bisexual woman, on the other hand, is allowed expression of masculine ascendancy because this is balanced, in society's eyes, by her sexual involvement with men. We therefore found a number of masculine bisexual women in our sample. Unmitigated communion (i.e., femininity) may be incongruous to both homosexual and bisexual women. A feminine individual finds it difficult to stand up to another individual (Bem, 1975), let alone an entire society. Bisexual and homosexual women have the character traits to do so. These women contravene social mores and some even flaunt their self-identity. Given that unmitigated masculinity or femininity may be anathema to the homosexual woman, she must temper her attributes to insure a psychological balance. Some succeed by repressing or suppressing both their masculinity and their femininity (i.e., undifferentiation); others are able to develop both sets of attributes to a high degree (i.e., androgyny). If this speculation is true, we may further expect that undifferentiated lesbians experience more anxiety about their erotic preference because of their repression or suppression. In fact, the average score for satisfaction with sexual activities was considerably lower for the undifferentiated lesbian ($\bar{x} = 3.5 \pm 1.60$) than for the androgynous lesbian ($\bar{x} = 4.4 \pm .52$).

The other outstanding finding in this report is that women who have, at some time in their lives, participated in a sexual experience with another woman possessed traits that distinguished them from the remainder of the sample. These women were more agentic (i.e., possessed more socially desirable masculine traits), more satisfied with their bodies and body functions, more satisfied with both their sexual activities and their biological sex, and more satisfied with themselves and their abilities.

In summary, sexual experiences are more related to personality than are erotic preference or self-labeling as homosexual, bisexual, or heterosexual. There is some aversion, displayed by homosexual and bisexual women, to unmitigated femininity. There is some indication that undifferentiated lesbians are significantly different from androgynous lesbians. Distinct subgroupings, although previously noted by a few researchers (e.g., Vance, 1978), have not received sufficient attention in the literature. Women who have experienced both same-sex and opposite-sex sexual experiences possess more socially desirable traits and report greater satisfaction with themselves and their bodies—characteristics indicative of greater psychological adjustment. The nature of this result is correlative and we are therefore forced to speculate whether experiencing sex with both a man and a woman somehow enriched subjects' lives and contributed to the development of those positively valued traits or whether, having a firm and secure basis, these women were allowed the freedom to expand their sexual experiences. The question is open to further research.

REFERENCES

Bem, S. The psychological measurement of androgyny. *Journal of Consulting & Clinical Psychology*, 1974, *42*, 155-162.

Bem, S. L. Sex-role adaptability: One consequence of psychological androgyny. *Journal of Personality & Social Psychology*, 1975, *31*, 634-643.

Blumstein, P. W. & Schwartz, P. Bisexuality: Some social psychological issues. *Journal of Social Issues*, 1977, *33*, 30-45.

Brooks, V. R. *Minority stress and lesbian women*. Lexington, MA: Lexington Books, 1981.

Buhrich, N. & McConaghy, N. Tests of gender feelings and behavior in homosexuality, transvestism and transsexualism. *Journal of Clinical Psychology*, 1979, *35*, 187-191.

Dailey, D. M. Adjustment of heterosexual and homosexual couples in pairing relationships: An exploratory study. *Journal of Sex Research*, 1979, *15*, 143-157.

Ellis, H. Sexual inversion. In *Studies in the psychology of sex* (Vol. 2). Philadelphia: Davis, 1915. (Originally published, 1901.)

Freud, S. [*Group psychology and the analysis of the ego*]. (J. Strachey, Ed. & trans.) London: Hogarth, 1959. (Originally published, 1922.)

Freund, K., Langevin, R., Laws, R. & Serber, M. Femininity and preferred partner age in homosexual males. *British Journal of Psychiatry*, 1974, *125*, 442-446.

Hooberman, R. E. Psychological androgyny, feminine gender identity and self-esteem in homosexual and heterosexual males. *Journal of Sex Research*, 1979, *15*, 306-315.

Kingdon, M. A. Lesbians. *Counseling Psychologist*, 1979, *8*, 44-45.

Krafft-Ebing, R. von *Psychopathia sexualis*. (H. E. Wedeck, trans.) New York: Putnam, 1965. (Originally published, 1886.)

MacDonald, A. P., Jr. Bisexuality: Some comments on research and theory. *Journal of Homosexuality*, 1981, *6*, 21-35.

Mucklow, B. M. & Phelan, G. K, Lesbian and traditional mothers' responses to adult response to child behavior and self-concept. *Psychological Reports*, 1979, *44*, 880-882.

Oberstone, A. K. & Sukoneck, H. Psychological adjustment and life style of single lesbians and single heterosexual women. *Psychology of Women Quarterly*, 1976, *1*, 172-188.

Reiss, B. F., Safer, J. & Yotive, W. Psychological test data on female homosexuality: A review of the literature. *Journal of Homosexuality*, 1974, *1*, 71-85.

Rosenberg, M. *Society and the adolescent self-image*. Princeton: Princeton University Press, 1965.

Secord, P. F. & Jourard, S. M. The appraisal of body-cathexis: Body cathexis and the self. *Journal of Consulting Psychology*, 1953, *17*, 343-347.

Siegelman, M. Adjustment of homosexual and heterosexual women: A cross-national replication. *Archives of Sexual Behavior*, 1979, *8*, 121-125.

Spence, J. T. & Helmreich, R. L. *Masculinity and femininity: Their psychological dimensions, correlates and antecedents*. Austin: University of Texas Press, 1978.

Spence, J. T., Helmreich, R. L. & Holohan, C. K. Negative and positive components of psychological masculinity and femininity and their relationships to self-reports of neurotic and acting out behaviors. *Journal of Personality & Social Psychology*, 1979, *37*, 1673-1682.

Spence, J. T., Helmreich, R. & Stapp, J. Ratings of self and peers on sex-role attributes and their relation to self-esteem and conceptions of masculinity and femininity. *Journal of Personality & Social Psychology*, 1975, *32*, 29-39.

Storms, M. D. Theories of sexual orientation. *Journal of Personality & Social Psychology*, 1980, *38*, 783-792.

Strassberg, D. S., Roback, H., Cunningham, J., McKee, E. & Larson, P. Psychopathology in self-identified female-to-male transsexuals, homosexuals, and heterosexuals. *Archives of Sexual Behavior*, 1979, *8*, 491-496.

Vance, B. K. Female homosexuality: A social psychological examination of attitudinal and etiological characteristics of different groups. *Dissertation Abstracts International*, 1978, *39*, 451B. (Order No. 7811075.)

A Comparison among Three Measures of Social Sex-Role

Sidney Greer Smith, MA

San Francisco State University

ABSTRACT. This study compared the De Cecco-Shively Social Sex-Role Inventory (DSI) with the Bem Sex-Role Inventory (BSRI) and the Personal Attributes Questionnaire (PAQ). The analysis, comparing methods of femininity and masculinity trait description, assessment, and scoring procedures among the instruments, was obtained by administering the three inventories to a sample of seventy-nine respondents. Femininity and masculinity scores in each inventory were then classified by assigning these scores to appropriate quadrants according to median splits. Additionally, Pearson product-moment correlations were calculated in order to compare the overall femininity and masculinity scores among each of the three measures. The BSRI and PAQ were found to be in somewhat closer agreement with each other than with the DSI. The DSI provides for measurement of a greater spectrum of types of variables, and also allows more flexibility regarding personal and situational factors associated with assessment of social sex-role.

The purpose of this study is to compare the De Cecco-Shively Social Sex-Role Inventory (DSI), a procedure for assessing social sex-role, with two similar measures of sex-role, the Bem Sex-Role Inventory (BSRI) and the Personal Attributes Questionnaire (PAQ). The DSI identifies conformity to and departure from feminine and masculine stereotypes. It has been developed in the Center for Research and Education in Sexuality (CERES). This research is designed to answer the following question: What degree of agreement exists among three measures of social sex-role currently used in psychological research?

Research literature relating to conceptualization and assessment of social sex-role has reflected several perspectives. In this study, social sex-role is considered one aspect of sexual identity. It refers to physical and psychological characteristics of individuals that are culturally associated with females or males. Social sex-role stereotypes are cultural expectations of appropriate physical and psychological character-

Mr. Smith was a research associate at CERES, at San Francisco State University, San Francisco, California 94132.

© 1983 by The Haworth Press, Inc. All rights reserved. *99*

istics for each sex. These characteristics are perceived by individuals as feminine or masculine. The following aspects of social sex-roles have been identified in current research (Shively, Rudolph & De Cecco, 1978): physical appearance, personality, mannerisms, speech, interests and habits.

Early conceptions of social sex-role were bipolar, and included the assumption that the presence of femininity implied the absence of masculinity and that the absence of femininity implied the presence of masculinity. Most psychological measures of social sex-role were based on the bipolar model (e.g., the masculinity-femininity scales of the Minnesota Multiphasic Personality Inventory and of the California Psychological Inventory). In recent research, femininity and masculinity have been measured on two independent continua. A man or woman can be seen as feminine, masculine, or both feminine and masculine. The Bem Sex-Role Inventory (Bem, 1974) contains sixty items for measuring personality traits (twenty characteristics each in "masculine," "feminine," and "neutral" categories). Bernard and Epstein (1978) compared androgyny scores for matched homosexual and heterosexual males using this procedure. Spence, Helmreich, and Stapp (1974, 1975) and Spence and Helmreich (1978) introduced a Personal Attributes Questionnaire that consisted of twenty-four bipolar attributes; they added the dimension of interests, sex-role valued items, and self-esteem measurements. Although Bem gave the label "androgynous" to personalities that reflected an equal degree of femininity and masculinity, Spence and her associates further distinguished between personalities with a high degree of femininity and masculinity ("androgynous") and those with a low degree of femininity and masculinity ("undifferentiated"). Wallace's study (Note 1) further expanded sex-role measurement by including various relationships, e.g., intimate, friendship or social, and work. His questionnaire instrument attempted to determine the relationships between sex-role "definitions and enactments" and sexual behavior. These studies, however, did not provide for measurement of appearance, speech and mannerisms. The De Cecco-Shively Social Sex-Role Measure (DSI) includes all identifiable aspects of social sex-role, and is situation-specific.

The sample was chosen on the basis of biological sex and sexual orientation mainly from a college population. The median age of the respondents was 24. The total sample of 79 respondents was divided into quadrants of heterosexual females ($n = 30$), homosexual females ($n = 10$), heterosexual males ($n = 24$) and homosexual males ($n = 15$). The sample contained a larger number of self-identified heterosexual respondents and, therefore, generalizations to homosexual respondents must be made with caution.

Instrumentation

The instruments were combined in the form of an interview questionnaire. Beginning with the informed consent form, which provided an explanation of the nature of the research project, the questionnaire included a background page, which contained questions about biological sex, age and sexual orientation. These questions were asked in order to identify the characteristics of the respondents. The research instrument consisted of three measures of social sex-role: the Bem Sex-Role Inventory (BSRI), the Personal Attributes Questionnaire (PAQ), and the De Cecco-Shively Social Sex-Role Inventory (DSI). The BSRI was designed to assess personality traits to determine the degree of androgyny, femininity and masculinity in individuals. The PAQ was designed by Spence and Helmreich also to assess personality characteristics. Like the BSRI, it yields a measure of androgyny. The De Cecco-Shively Inventory was designed to assess mannerisms, speech, and appearance as well as personality characteristics. All three measures indicate the individual's self-perceptions of traits associated with femininity and masculinity.

Bem Sex-Role Inventory. For the sixty personality characteristics on the BSRI, the respondent indicates, on a scale of one to seven, how pertinent to her/himself each characteristic is. The respondent receives a femininity score, a masculinity score, and a social desirability score. The femininity and masculinity scores represent the mean for all feminine and masculine items, respectively, Both means range from one to seven. This revised method divides subjects into one of four groups; high masculine-low feminine, low masculine-high feminine, androgynous (high masculine-high feminine) and undifferentiated (low masculine-low feminine) according to median splits for the masculine and feminine scales.

Personal Attributes Questionnaire. The 24 bipolar attributes in the PAQ are rated on a five-point scale. The scales are feminine-valued, masculine-valued, and sex specific. The total score for each of three scales is determined by summing points for the items. For the PAQ, as for the BSRI, the individual score falls into one of four femininity-masculinity categories.

The latest scoring procedure for the PAQ involves the median split method, described by Spence and Helmreich (1978), as follows:

> In instances in which more than one of the individual scales on the PAQ are found to be correlated with other variables, a method of combining scale scores is necessary if the nature of the conjoint relationship is to be determined. The approach we have adopted

for purposes of both description and prediction is first to determine for a total sample (females and males combined) or a normative group the median scores on the M and F scales. Then the individuals are classified by means of a 2 by 2 table according to their position above or below the median on the two scales. (p. 35)

This scoring procedure results in four mutually exclusive classifications of sex-roles.

De Cecco-Shively Social Sex-Role Inventory. There are four categories of items in this inventory: personality, appearance, speech, and mannerisms. Respondents are asked to take the following four steps: (1) List characteristics of their personality, appearance, speech, and mannerisms; (2) Give themselves an overall rating for femininity and masculinity, using two four-point rating scales ranging from one ("not at all") to four ("very"); (3) Rate each listed characteristic for femininity using the four-point femininity scale; and (4) Rate each listed characteristic for masculinity using the four-point masculinity scale.

Analysis of Data

First, the respondent's BSRI femininity, masculinity, and social desirability scores wre recorded. Individual scores could consequently be classified into one of four quadrants previously mentioned. Second, respondents' PAQ female-valued, male-valued, and sex specific scores were recorded, using exactly the same procedure. Third, the DSI scores (self-ratings) were recorded, represented by a median femininity rating and a median masculinity rating for the categories of personality, appearance, speech and mannerisms. From these scores, an overall femininity score and an overall masculinity score were calculated for each respondent. As with the BSRI and the PAQ sections, respondents' scores were then classified into one of four quadrants.

Two procedures were used to determine the degree of agreement among the three measures of social sex-role: (1) assigning respondents to one of four quadrants, using median splits, and (2) obtaining Pearson product-moment correlations for respondents' femininity and masculinity scores on each instrument.

Results

Table 1 shows the medians for all three measures. These medians were used to assign respondents to the appropriate quadrants for each measure. Table 2 shows the comparison of the three measures for agreement on assignment of respondents to the various quadrants. As shown in Table 2, there is considerably more agreement between the BSRI

TABLE 1*

MEDIANS FOR THREE MEASURES
OF SOCIAL SEX-ROLE

	Femininity	Masculinity
BSRI	4.850	4.948
PAQ	2.898	2.653
DSI	2.640	2.758

*Since the DSI has no assessment corresponding to
the sex-specific items (PAQ) and social
desirability items (BSRI), comparisons using those
items were not made.

TABLE 2

OVERALL COMPARISON OF THREE MEASURES

	Agreement	Disagreement
BSRI vs. DSI	26 (33%)	53 (67%)
PAQ vs. DSI	27 (34%)	52 (66%)
BSRI vs. PAQ	47 (59%)	32 (41%)

and PAQ than between either of these measures and the DSI. Table 3 shows agreement for the three measures on femininity and masculinity. As shown in Table 3, there is a relatively higher agreement between the BSRI and PAQ than between either of these measures and the DSI. Additionally, the BSRI and PAQ are more closely related on femininity than on overall agreement (72 % vs. 59% overall agreement respectively). Also, both the BSRI and PAQ are more closely related to the DSI on femininity alone than overall (62% agreement vs. 33% for the BSRI, and 62% agreement vs. 34% for the PAQ). There is greater agreement between the BSRI and PAQ on masculinity than between each of these measures and the DSI (81% agreement vs. 61% and 57% respectively).

Both the BSRI and PAQ are more closely related to the DSI on masculinity alone than to overall agreement (61% agreement vs. 33% and 57% vs. 34% respectively). There is less disagreement on femininity than on masculinity between, on one hand, the BSRI and PAQ

TABLE 3

COMPARISON OF THREE MEASURES ON FEMININITY AND MASCULINITY

| | Femininity | | | Masculinity | |
	Agreement	Disagreement		Agreement	Disagreement
BSRI vs. DSI	49 (62%)	30 (38%)	BSRI vs. DSI	48 (61%)	31 (39%)
PAQ vs. DSI	49 (62%)	30 (38%)	PAQ vs. DSI	44 (57%)	35 (43%)
BSRI vs. PAQ	57 (72%)	22 (28%)	BSRI vs. PAQ	64 (81%)	15 (19%)

and, on the other hand, the DSI (10% of femininity vs. 20% and 24%, respectively, on masculinity). As shown in Table 3 there is a relatively higher agreement on masculinity than on femininity between the BSRI and PAQ (81% vs. 72%).

To assess the reliability of results obtained by means of the median split method, the scores for femininity and the scores for masculinity on the three measures were correlated and the level of significance of the correlations determined.[1] Table 4 represents this analysis.

As shown in Table 4 the BSRI and DSI show a highly significant correlation on femininity ($r = .2855$, $p \leq .005$). For these measures, there is also a highly significant correlation on masculinity ($r = .2639$, $p \leq .009$). There is an even higher and more significant correlation between the PAQ and DSI on femininity ($r = .3319$, $p \leq .001$). The correlation between the PAQ and DSI for masculinity almost reaches an acceptable level of significance ($r = .1778$, $p \leq .059$). Agreement reaches a higher level of significance on femininity than on masculinity between the BSRI and DSI ($p \leq .005$ and $p \leq .009$ respectively), and there is also more significance for femininity than for masculinity between the PAQ and DSI ($p \leq .001$ and $p \leq .059$, respectively). The results of both analyses (quartile median split method and Pearson r correlation method) are consistent. The correlations fall in the same direction as the percentages of agreement in Tables 2 and 3 based on the median split method.

Discussion

The question arises as to why there was consistently more agreement found between the PAQ and the BSRI than between either of these instruments and the DSI. There are several possible explanations. The

---

[1]The author gratefully acknowledges the assistance of Randall Jones in programming the computer for this analysis.

DSI requires respondents to take four steps, which is a more detailed procedure than the one-step process required in the other two measures. It also requires respondents to describe four aspects of the self, including both the physical and psychological: appearance, mannerisms, speech and personality. The other measures are limited mostly to psychological, i.e., personality traits. This is an important difference, since an individual's perception of femininity and masculinity is most likely a composite of both the physical and the psychological.

In addition, the BSI and PAQ have a predetermined list of traits which does not vary from respondent to respondent. The DSI, however, is specific to each individual because the lists of characteristics are generated by respondents themselves. The BSRI and PAQ also do not vary from situation to situation since they are apparently based on the assumption that individuals possess a stable group of traits. On the DSI, the characteristics listed can vary from situation to situation since they are reported for particular interactions.

Some of the greater agreement of the BSRI and PAQ may be attributed to similarities in scaling. There is more possibility for agreement between the more extended scales (the seven-point scale of the

TABLE 4

CORRELATIONS (PEARSON PRODUCT-MOMENT) FOR
FEMININITY AND MASCULINITY SCORES
ON THE THREE MEASURES

	BSRI M	PAQ F	PAQ M	DSI F	DSI M
BSRI F	$r = -.1490$	$r = .6631$	$r = -.1650$	$r = .2855$	$r = -.0804$
	$p = .095$	$p = .001**$	$p = .073$	$p = .005*$	$p = .241$
BSRI M		$r = -.0662$	$r = .7451$	$r = -.0166$	$r = .2639$
		$p = .281$	$p = .001**$	$p = .446$	$p = .009*$
PAQ F			$r = .0069$	$r = .3319$	$r = -.0764$
			$p = .476$	$p = .001**$	$p = .252$
PAQ M				$r = .0176$	$r = .1778$
				$p = .439$	$p = .059$
DSI F					$r = .0390$
					$p = .366$

* significant at $p < .01$ ** significant at $p < .001$

BSRI and the five-point scale of the PAQ) than between either of these scales and the more attenuated four-point scale of the DSI. Some of the disagreement in scores of the BSRI and PAQ with the DSI scores may be due to variation in the composition of the samples. Whereas the former two measures were developed using college undergraduates whose ages averaged eighteen or nineteen, the median age of the respondents in this study was twenty-four. Older respondents would probably find the refinements and greater complexity of the DSI a more accurate description of their sex-roles, while young undergraduates would prefer the unilinear procedure of the BSRI and PAQ.

Why was there more agreement on femininity than on masculinity between the DSI and the other two measures? One can speculate that the greater number of self-identified homosexual males in this study tended to inflate femininity scores on all measures, thus making it possible to have more agreement on femininity.

The disagreements between the DSI, on one hand, and the BSRI and PAQ, on the other, raise a basic theoretical question about the wisdom of assessing social sex-role characteristics in the abstract (without situational context) and as fixed traits of individuals. "Roles" denote interactions between two or more individuals and interactions denote relationships. Femininity and masculinity, therefore, perhaps should be considered aspects of relationships, rather than aspects of isolated individuals. Femininity and masculinity are, perhaps, nothing more than broad labels applied to diverse perceptions and expectations out of which individuals construct their relationships. It is very likely that individuals have different expectations for different relationships and, therefore, conduct themselves in different ways. Thus social sex-roles are products of relationships as much as they are their substance.

REFERENCE NOTE

1. Wallace, D. H. "Sex-role Behavior and Sexual Functioning." Unpublished research proposal. Human Sexuality Program at University of California Medical School, San Francisco, 1976.

REFERENCES

Bakan, D. *The duality of human existence*. Chicago: Rand McNally, 1966.
Bem, S. L. The measurement of psychological androgyny. *Journal of Consulting and Clinical Psychology,* 1974, *42,* 155-162.
Bernard, L. C. and Epstein, D. J. Androgyny scores of matched homosexual and heterosexual males. *Journal of Homosexuality,* 1978, *4*(2), 169-178.
Shively, M. G., Rudolph, J. R. and De Cecco, J. P. The identification of the social sex-role stereotypes. *Journal of Homosexuality,* 1978, *3*(3), 225-234.

Spence, J. T., Helmreich, R. and Stapp, J. The Personal Attributes Questionnaire: A measure of sex-role stereotypes and masculinity-femininity. *JSAS Catalogue of Selected Documents in Psychology,* 1974, *4,* 127.

Spence, J. T., Helmreich, R. and Stapp, J. Ratings of self and peers on sex-role attributes and their relation to self-esteem and conceptions of masculinity and femininity. *Journal of Personality and Social Psychology,* 1975, *32,* 29-39.

Spence, J. T. and Helmreich, R. *Masculinity and femininity: Their psychological dimensions, correlates, and antecedents.* Austin & London: University of Texas Press, 1978.

I.D No. b13635864

UNIVERSITY OF BRADFORD
LIBRARY

1 2 OCT 2010

ACCESSION No. 0400837346
CLASS No.
LOCATION